HOORAY FOR PEACE, HURRAH FOR WAR

THE UNITED STATES DURING WORLD WAR I

The Library of American History
General Editor: John Anthony Scott

HOORAY FOR PEACE, HURRAH FOR WAR

THE UNITED STATES DURING WORLD WAR I

Steven Jantzen

Facts On File
New York • Oxford

181- 93

Hooray for Peace, Hurrah for War

Facts On File, Inc.
460 Park Avenue South
New York NY 10016
USA

Facts On File Limited
Collins Street
Oxford OX4 1XJ
United Kingdom

Library of Congress Cataloging-in-Publication Data

Jantzen, Steven, 1941
    Hooray for peace, hurrah for war : the United States during World War I / Steven Jantzen.
      p.   cm. — (The Library of American history)
    Reprint. Originally published: New York: Knopf, 1972, c 1971.
    Includes bibliographical references (p.   ) and index.
    Summary: Traces the impact of World War I on American society, from the spirited organization of the "home front" to the social conditions and contributions of poor immigrants, middle classes, and the wealthy.
    ISBN 0-8160-2453-7
    1. World War, 1914–1918—United States.   2. United States—1913–1921.   3. United States—Social conditions—1865–1918. [1. World War, 1914–1918—United States. 2. United States--History— 1913–1921.   3. United States—Social conditions—1865–1918.] I. Title. II. Series
    D619.J35 1991
    940.3'73—dc20   90-13916

A British CIP catalogue record for this book is available from the British Library.

Facts On File books are available at special discounts when purchased in bulk quantities for businesses, associations, institutions or sales promotion. Please call our Special Sales Department in New York at 212/683-2244 (dial 800/322-8755 except in NY, AK, or HI) or in Oxford at 865/728399.

Text design by Donna Sinisgalli
Jacket design by Solonay/Mitchell Associates
Composition by Facts On File, Inc.
Manufactured by The Maple-Vail Book Manufacturing Group
Printed in the United States of America

10 9 8 7 6 5 4 3 2 1

This book is printed on acid-free paper.

CONTENTS

PREFACE

Millions of American young people passing through our schools and colleges learn their United States history almost exclusively from standard textbooks. Growing dissatisfaction with these texts was eloquently voiced when Frances Fitzgerald published *America Revised: History Schoolbooks in the Twentieth Century* in 1979. High school history texts, Fitzgerald charged, are supremely dull and uninteresting. They fail to hold the attention of young people or to fire their imagination. United States history ought to arouse wonder, compassion and delight, but these books turn it into a crashing bore. One of the reasons for this, she said, is that the texts do not often draw upon the marvelous original sources that this nation inherits, which constitute the lifeblood of history, and which are indispensable to its study, no matter what the age of the student.

Efforts to find alternatives to the traditional texts began some years before Fitzgerald's book appeared. One of these was an initiative that Alfred A. Knopf launched in 1966. The result was the publication, during the years 1967–77, of an historical series designed for the use of high school students and of undergraduates and entitled the Living History Library. In all, fifteen volumes were published in this series. Each book was written by a distinguished historian or teacher. Each told the story of a different period or topic in American history—the Colonial Period, the American Revolution, the black experience in the Civil

War, the cowboy in the West, the Great Depression, and so on. Each was based upon original sources, woven throughout into the framework of the narrative. Ordinary people who witnessed historical events and participated in historical struggles provided their own testimony and told their own story both in word and song. The series presented the American experience through the medium of a new literary art form. People long dead and struggles long past came to life again in the present.

The historical and literary value of these books has not diminished with the passage of time. On the contrary, the need for books such as these is greater today than it has ever been before. Innumerable important topics in our history await treatment of this type. Facts On File is happy to publish new and updated editions of the Living History Library books as part of its Library of American History.

This book recounts the American experience during World War I, 1914–1919, at home and on the battle front. The canvas is a large one; upon it the author captures and recreates life in a time of crisis. We get to know all kinds of people: Archie Taber, who toughened himself by bathing in ice-cold water and left Princeton to join the American Ambulance Service in Europe; Quentin Roosevelt, who became a pilot and was shot down over the German lines; Emma Goldman, who spoke quietly to jeering soldiers and told them that the war was wrong; Ernest Meyer, who was drafted into the army against his will and then refused an order to put on the uniform. We learn about the sinking of the *Lusitania* in the words of terrified passengers; we watch the ship go down through the eyes of the German U-boat commander who sank it. Soldiers battle and die in the trenches of France and mutilated survivors throng the hospitals. Peace comes with the image of German and American soldiers throwing away their guns and embracing each other as brothers.

HOORAY FOR PEACE, HURRAH FOR WAR

THE UNITED STATES DURING WORLD WAR I

1

ARE YOU SORRY FOR THESE LADS?

For New Yorkers, this hot Monday morning in May 1914 was something of a holiday—though a sad one. Business offices were closed until noon. School children were lined up along the curb, watching their teachers nervously for the signal to sing "Nearer My God to Thee." All around them, thousands of spectators crowded the sidewalks. The men's hats were off; the women wore black.

Silently the crowd looked on as a band played Chopin's funeral march and a procession of seventeen coffins—drawn by horses and wrapped in American flags—moved slowly past. In a carriage following the coffins rode the president, Woodrow Wilson. A reporter for the *New York Times* wrote:

The President was silent and very grave. Months ago he had foreseen all this—the flag-wrapped coffins, the sorrowing families of the dead, the mourning crowd. His square jaw was set as he rode in the open carriage and his eyes were misty as he repeatedly raised his hat and bowed to the multitude.

The 17 dead men were sailors and marines killed two weeks before in an American attack on the city of Vera Cruz, Mexico. Following many months of tension between

1

Mexico and the United States, Mexican military officials had imprisoned a group of American sailors. When asked to apologize formally for the deed with a 21 gun salute to the American flag, they had refused. In retaliation, President Wilson had ordered the seizure of Vera Cruz, Mexico's major seaport. The attack had cost the American troops only light casualties, but the few who had lost their lives were now receiving the nation's full tribute.

The funeral procession stopped at the Brooklyn Navy Yard, and President Wilson stepped down from his carriage. When taps had sounded over the 17 dead, the president addressed the hushed crowd. He expressed greater pride than sorrow. "Are you sorry for these lads?" he asked.

Are you sorry for the way they will be remembered? Does it not quicken your pulses to think of the list of them? I hope to God none of you may join the list, but if you do, you will join an immortal company.

So while we are profoundly sorrowful and while there goes out of our heart a very deep and affectionate sympathy for the friends and relatives of these lads who for the rest of their lives shall mourn them, though with a touch of pride, we know why we do not go away from this occasion cast down but with our heads lifted and our eyes on the future of this country, with absolute confidence of how it will be worked out . . .

"With absolute confidence" and "with a touch of pride"— these words expressed the prevailing spirit of America in the spring of 1914. Americans felt proud of their past and confident of their future. They believed their nation could do no wrong in the world. This sense of national righteousness strongly impressed Stephen Graham, an English author who traveled the country in 1914, seeking to capture in a book something of the peculiar spirit of America. Graham observed:

It is all important to the American that he feels he lives and dies for the Right, for the moral virtues. The glory of the wars which the Americans have fought in their history is not only that they, the Americans, were victorious, but that they were morally right before they ever started out to fight.

Graham trekked on foot from New York to Chicago, talking with everyone he met along the way—coal miners, farmers, fishermen and schoolboys. He found that Americans believed, above everything else, in the greatness of their country. "The chief characteristic of America," he wrote, "is an immense patriotism . . . It is a real, hearty patriotic fervour, the deepest thing in an American. It is something that cannot be shaken."

Perhaps he was right. From an early age, American children were taught to serve both their country and mankind. In 1914, students in many of the nation's schools were required by their state legislature to recite a pledge that they would always remember to serve their fellow citizens. It was a long and complicated pledge, that began:

I am a citizen of America and an heir to all her greatness and renown. The health and happiness of my own body depend upon each muscle and nerve and drop of blood doing its work in its place. So the health and happiness of my country depend upon each citizen doing his work in his place . . .

Repeated as often as it was, this pledge must have seeped into the thinking of everyone in the class. Perhaps it was the spirit behind the pledge that inspired the following charitable note of June 1914 to the *New York Herald:*

Enclosed please find a check for $3, a fund which a sewing class of six little girls saved to have an outing in Prospect Park, but which they decided would be better spent if donated to the Herald *Free Ice Fund.*

In 1914, ice was a common necessity of life. No one had yet heard of an electric refrigerator. To keep food from spoiling, people relied on a metal-lined wooden chest with an upper compartment that held a large chunk of ice and a lower compartment for food—popularly known as an ice box. Refrigeration by this method cost only pennies a week, but they were pennies the poor could ill afford. Children of the very poor often had to eat rotting food and drink warm, sour milk. It was to correct this situation that the *Herald* Free Ice Fund gave away blocks of ice to the needy. The *Herald* created the Ice Fund and the girls' sewing class gave $3 for much the same reason that school teachers made their children recite a humanitarian pledge. They all wanted to show that they were good Americans by demonstrating their willingness to serve the "less fortunate."

In 1914, there were millions of poor in America. Many of them were immigrants from the countries of southern and eastern Europe—Italy, Greece, Russia and Poland. Like the English, Germans and Irish who originally settled this country, they had come in search of a better life. They came without knowing anything more about America than its reputation as the land of political freedom and economic opportunity.

At first, life in America offered none of the joy and abundance that the immigrants had dreamed about. At Ellis Island, the immigrants' gateway to New York, officials treated the weary voyagers like cattle, herding them into giant stalls, checking their bodies for diseases and their past lives for crime and immorality. "Have you ever been arrested?" one inspector asked Stephen Graham. "Do you believe a man may possess more than one wife at a time? . . . How much money have you got?" When they had passed through the ranks of inspectors, the immigrants were released from the human cattleyard at Ellis Island only to enter into the swarming slums of New York's East Side. This is what those slums looked like to Stephen Graham in 1914:

The New York slums are slums at the intensest. The buildings, great frames of rags and dirt, hang over the busy street below, and are wildly alive from base to summit. All day long the bedding hangs out at the windows or on the iron fire-escapes attached to the houses. Women are shouting and children are crying on the extraordinary stairs which lead from room to room and story to story in the vast

The author's mother and her cousins on a patriotic holiday about 1914. (Credit: Ernest Lauckhardt)

honeycomb of dens. On the sidewalk is a rough crowd speaking all tongues . . . Lithuanian and Polish boys are rushing after one another with toy pistols, the girls are going round and round the barber's pole, singing and playing, with hands joined . . .

Every year, for the 10 years ending in 1914, an average of 100,000 new immigrants crowded into the dingy tenements of New York and worked amidst pounding machinery and blinding fumes for 10 to 14 hours a day as factory hands, stevedores, construction workers. A good wage for a man who couldn't speak English was 20 cents an hour. Another 900,000 immigrants a year packed special labor trains out of New York and found their way into the tenement rooms and factory jobs of Boston, Pittsburgh, Chicago, Denver and San Francisco. A much smaller number went south, where the meanest work was already being done by blacks. In all, a million immigrants a year sought opportunity in American cities. Few of them found anything in their first year but bewilderment, loneliness and endless toil.

One might expect, then, that most immigrants wished they'd never left home. But it wasn't so. "Most people who go to America," reported Stephen Graham at the end of his travels, "are disillusioned sooner or later but they re-catch their dreams and illusions . . . They have become Americans, and have a stake in America, and are ready to back the New World against anything in the Old." How could this happen? How could an immigrant still believe in America after being handled so roughly at Ellis Island and ever afterward? Perhaps it was because he heard countless stories of immigrants like himself who finally succeeded. There was, for example, a Greek in South Bend, Indiana who told Stephen Graham how he had scraped together enough money to buy a soda fountain and could now easily afford to treat Graham to a dish of his own "Yankee Doodle" ice cream.

In seeking to make a new life for themselves, immigrants gave new life and strength to their adopted country. President Wilson expressed this idea in his speech about the 17 sailors killed at Vera Cruz.

Notice how truly these men [the Very Cruz dead] were of our blood. I mean of our American blood, which is not drawn from any one country, which is not drawn from any one stock, which is not drawn from any one language of the modern world; but free men everywhere have sent their sons and their brothers and their daughters to this country in order to make that great compounded nation which consists of all the sturdy elements of the whole globe.

If the leader of his country believed in him, the immigrant believed in America above all because so many other people seemed to believe in it. The native-born white American whether he ran the bank in Tulsa, Oklahoma or grew apples in Rutland, Vermont believed without question that in America anything was possible to the man who tried. Whatever a man might pay for the privilege in moral or physical distress, it was still a proud thing to be an American in 1914. Consider all that the nation had built in a short time, was building then and undoubtedly would build in the future. Look, for example, at the Woolworth Building, in 1914 the tallest office building in the world. In the opinion of *Harper's Weekly*, a popular magazine of the day, nothing better showed the genius of American enterprise than this gigantic structure rising high over Manhattan.

The Woolworth Building . . . well represents the present enterprising century. Towering 750 feet above the street, it is the highest structure ever reared by the hand of man save only the Eiffel Tower in Paris. Twenty-eight high-speed elevators are required to handle the traffic of its fifty-five stories. The owner of this $13,000,000 property, Mr. F. W. Woolworth, began his business career as a clerk in a small upstate city a little over thirty years ago. To-day he is at the head of a company controlling a chain of about 600 five-and-ten cent stores, which prosper because they help the masses to buy economically in these times of the high cost of living.

Thus the Woolworth Building may be regarded as a vast monument to Thrift, and to the opportunity which is another name for America in this glorious twentieth century.

Chugging past the Woolworth Building went hundreds of other proofs of an America on the move. In 1908, Henry Ford had marketed a black box on wheels that was sturdier and more reliable than any automobile the world had ever seen. The Model-T Ford was also one of the world's most awkward looking cars, but it got people up hills, over bumps and through mud as well as a horse and buggy—and it cost only $825, within reach of all but the poorest American families. By 1912, about a million machines, many of them Fords, were slowly forcing the old horse-drawn buggies off the road. During the next two years alone, another million cars rolled out of America's factories.

By 1914 the automobile had ceased to be a curiosity; on the other hand, spotting a "flying machine" or "aeroplane" in the sky was still something to talk about for days at a time. The very daring could go to the town fair grounds and ride in the single passenger seat behind the pilot in a flimsy, two-winged plane that did between 40 and 60 miles per hour. The last daredevil to attempt a transcontinental flight from New York to San Francisco had to stop 68 times and took 49 days to reach his destination. Even so, people were so sure about the airplane's possibilities that they dared to imagine a day when travel by plane would be a matter of course. In *Harper's Weekly* a writer made the bold prediction that planes of the future would hold as many as seven passengers. He also proposed an easy way to land planes in cities—simply connect the rooftops of adjacent buildings and level all chimneys. Planes landing on this rooftop runway could be stored in a many-floored parking garage.

There was also confident talk of a day when the hydroplane "America" would cross the Atlantic. To prove that it could be done, enthusiasts pointed to the world's record over-water flight—152 miles over the Hudson River.

Yes, in 1914 America boasted the tallest skyscraper, the largest number of automobiles and the greatest confidence in the world. In addition, its women considered themselves more privileged than the women of any other country in the world. Though her bathing suit covered everything but face, neck, hands and feet and she could not smoke cigarettes, the American woman could ride a bicycle, drive an

Λ Rio touring car on a country road in Massachu-setts, 1911. (Credit: William Jantzen)

automobile and hold a job without losing her place in respectable society. In addition, women in most states west of the Missouri River could vote. In other states where women were still barred from voting, the cause of women's suffrage was picking up momentum. In New York in 1912, a parade of 10,000 suffragettes—as women who campaigned to win the right to vote were called—met an unexpectedly warm reception. Of the million specta- tors, only three men heckled the lady marchers, and they were arrested for causing a public disturbance. A man who marched with the women in the parade expressed the benign mood of the occasion in four short lines of verse:

> *It was a comfort as we marched to*
> *See the policemen smile,*
> *And it was one big good-natured*
> *Laugh the whole three mile.*

Such peaceful demonstration was in sharp contrast to the violence of a similar movement in England. There, suffragettes burned mail boxes, crippled the king's racing horses, slashed paintings in the Royal Gallery, even broke into the Egyptian mummy cases in the Royal Museum to publicize their crusade.

In addition to the vote, young women in America had more freedom than British or French girls to experiment with new and daring dance steps. In resorts along the East Coast, turkey-trotting to rhythmic banjo music was be- coming more fashionable than the waltz. Though tame by present standards, the tight embraces and impassioned music that characterized the turkey trot and other new dances shocked some of the older generation. Young visi- tors to the country, however, were thrilled. A girl in her teens described a Frenchman's reaction to the turkey trot:

> *A young Frenchman I met at Hampton Beach last winter*
> *just raved over it. He was dancing every moment he could*
> *find a girl to dance with. He said we Americans were so*
> *charming, so ingenuous; that in France no one would dare*
> *to suggest such a dance among nice people; yet over here it*
> *was quite all right.*

The self-image of American girls was just another expression of the daring and confidence felt by the American nation as a whole in the spring of 1914. After all, compared with the nations of Europe, America was a young country. As such, she had great ambitions, sweeping ideals and the vitality to carry them through. She had a heroic image of herself as the one nation that could show the world the blessings of a democratic government. At the time, of course, there was no Peace Corps or any other such foreign aid program. But Americans believed that other countries would progress on their own, so long as they were guided by the supreme example of progress set by the United States. Thus, simply by enriching themselves and improving their own democracy, American citizens were lighting the way to a world in which everyone would vote, own an automobile and be at peace with his brother.

At least one American had hopes that a lasting peace could be achieved in his own lifetime—and he had only a few more years to live. Andrew Carnegie had come to America from Scotland as a young man. At his first job, he had earned $1.20 a week. But before long, by luck and hard work, he accumulated enough cash to invest in the manufacture of steel. In 1914, at the age of 79, Carnegie had over a billion dollars, and he had already given millions away for a multitude of worthy causes. His last and dearest ambition was to prevent nations from ever again going to war. Toward this end, he financed the building of a massive palace in the Netherlands called the Hague Peace Palace, where international disputes were to be settled by the decision of a board of judges. Carnegie hoped that his Peace Palace, plus a 10 million dollar "Endowment for International Peace," would be enough to prevent wars. As for his own country, there was no possibility of war. The United States, Carnegie said in 1911, "bears a charmed life and all works for her good."

She has not an enemy in the world, nor need she have. The rulers have no cause of complaint against her. The masses of the people in all civilized lands see in her the standard to which they fondly hope to attain and they love her. Hence an army and navy, maintained at present

*standard, are ample and more than ample. We have no
enemies, all nations are our friends and we are friends of
all.*

For three days in April 1914 Mexico seemed the only
exception to Carnegie's statement. And even this minor
incident was being settled over a conference table as
President Wilson eulogized the 17 men killed at Vera
Cruz. It is true that labor disputes of savage intensity had
erupted in many parts of the country, but still, many
Americans in the spring of 1914 might be pardoned for the
impression that they lived in a peaceful, untroubled world.
It seemed so peaceful that the headlines of the day in the
New York Herald of June 18, 1914, carried nothing of
greater import than stories of a runaway horse in New
Jersey, the capsizing of a rowboat on the Hudson River
and the damage suit of an exhibitor of prize dogs. Then,
on June 29, 1914, a similarly obscure headline ran across
the *Herald*'s 10th page:

ASSASSINS KILL ARCHDUKE FRANCIS FERDINAND HEIR TO THE THRONE OF AUSTRIA, AND HIS WIFE DUCHESS OF HOHENBERG, IN BOSNIAN CAPITAL

The assassination occurred far away in Sarajevo, a
remote town in Austria-Hungary that few Americans had
ever heard of. It was interesting news but probably no
more significant for Americans, people thought, than the
capsizing of a rowboat. Thus, toward the beginning of
summer 1914, people in the United States went about
their business, unaware of a future in which thousands of
boys then in school would meet the same fate as the Vera
Cruz dead, oblivious to the fact that their peaceful world
and their broad optimism would be totally shattered
within the next five years.

2

MURDER AT SARAJEVO

A gypsy once told Austrian Archduke Franz Ferdinand his fortune. Some day, she said, he would be the cause of a world war. That day came on Sunday, June 28, 1914.

It was a splendid day in Sarajevo, a town of gleaming white houses and noisy Turkish bazaars in the southern corner of the Austro-Hungarian empire. The peaceful Miljacka River glittered under a dazzling golden sun. Running alongside the river, the Appel Quay, Sarajevo's main street, was alive with noise, color and confusion. Great pots of flowers lined the sidewalks. Oriental carpets hung from the shop windows. Men and boys in red Turkish hats and loose-fitting white shirts joked with women and girls in fancily embroidered blue and scarlet skirts. A car's horn tooted and thousands of tanned, laughing faces turned to catch a glimpse of the heir to the Austrian throne, Archduke Franz Ferdinand, and his wife, Soferl, as they drove in an open car down the Appel Quay.

At the same time, a thin, grim-faced youth with a hairline mustache thrust his hand into his jacket pocket and stepped to the edge of the road. The crowd, happily waving at the archduke's oncoming car, failed to notice him.

Elsewhere on this beautiful Sunday in late June, sounds of gaiety and laughter bubbled up from the cobbled streets and outdoor cafes of villages and towns all over Europe. No one talked of the possibility of war.

On this quiet Sunday, it was easy to forget that a general European war had been threatening for 50 years—and threatened even now. All the major powers of Europe had long been involved in formal alliances that, under certain circumstances, would oblige them to go to war. These alliances had their origins deep in Europe's troubled history of constant diplomatic scheming and periodic wars. The kings and princes, kaisers and czars who once ruled Europe with almost absolute power used to play at war as at a favorite sport. Complicating their antagonisms were a series of intricate intermarriages that bound one royal family to another and played as strong a role in the struggle for power as armies and ships of war. Entering the 20th century, Europe's royalty were still formally related by the most intimate family ties. Thus, in 1914, the czar of Russia was cousin to both the king of England and the kaiser of Germany.

But even these family relations were split down the middle by long-standing rivalries between nations. Russia and France clashed regularly with Germany over conflicting claims to colonies in Africa, Asia and the Middle East. The Russian czar therefore contracted an alliance with the republic of France against his cousin, the German kaiser. In retaliation, the kaiser arranged an alliance between Imperial Germany and the sprawling empire of Austria-Hungary.

The division of Europe resulting from these two alliances contained the seeds of an international war of staggering proportions. If, for example, something happened that led Russia to declare war on Austria-Hungary, then Germany, as Austria-Hungary's ally, was pledged to go to war against Russia. At the same time, France, as Russia's ally, was pledged to fight Germany. England would come in to support France, and Italy would come in to support Germany. Thus a quarrel between any two nations vitally concerned the whole of Europe.

As a result of all this tension, the different nations of Europe were making frantic arrangements in 1914 to insure military preparedness. Never had Europe been so thoroughly equipped for war as in 1914. British and German harbors were jammed with battleships and destroyers, and still the factories strained to turn out more. One French machine gun had the capacity to massacre a platoon of Germans in a matter of seconds, but one machine gun was not enough; there had to be thousands. Germany's giant cannons would be able to turn to rubble any French village on the map, but ways were still being sought to increase their destructive power.

Danger signals were everywhere in the former secret and now public preparations for the anticipated struggle. In Germany, for example, American author Theodore Dreiser observed a gawking, bow-legged boy lounging on a railroad platform, a garland of flowers hanging rakishly down his back.

I was looking at his collarless shirt, his big feet and hands and his bow legs, when I heard a German in the next seat remark to his neighbor, "He won't look like that long."

"Three months—he'll be fine."

They went on reading their papers and I fell to wondering what they could mean.

At the next station were five more yokels, all similarly crowned, and around them a bevy of rosy, healthy village girls. These five, constituting at once a crowd and a center of attention, were somewhat more assured—more swaggering—than the lone youth we had seen.

"What is that?" I asked the man over the seat. "What are they doing?"

"They've been drawn for the army," he replied. "All over Germany the young men are being drawn like this."

"Do they begin to serve at once?"

"At once . . ."

At another railroad station farther on, Dreiser watched with foreboding as a troop of German soldiers strutted past:

Around a corner a full regiment suddenly came into view. They swung past me and crossed a bridge over the Rhine, their brass helmets glittering. Their trousers were gray and their jackets red, and they marched with a slap, slap, slap of their feet that was positively ominous. Every man's body was as erect as a poker; every man's gun was carried with almost loving grace over his shoulder.

Only a few miles away, across the German border, French soldiers practiced stabbing their bayonets into imaginary Germans. Across the channel to the north, English soldiers were learning how to feed bullets into the deadliest weapon yet invented, the machine gun. Far to the east, in the mountain passes of Russia, horses' hooves pounded against the hard, rocky ground, and Cossacks' sabers flashed in the sun. And in their military headquarters in the various capitals of Europe, generals pored over maps and plotted their strategies of war. The French generals were certain they could break through the center of the German lines and push on to Berlin. Russian generals envisioned teeming masses of peasant soldiers driving toward Germany. German generals, faced with the possibility of war on two fronts, counted on smashing France in one swift, irresistible sweep through Belgium and then taking on the slower-moving Russians.

The war everyone dreaded but no one knew how to prevent had almost happened before—many times. In 1907, it had almost resulted from a French and German quarrel over who was to control Morocco. It had almost happened again in 1908 when Austria-Hungary angered Russia by annexing a piece of territory that Russia's friend Serbia sought for herself. There was a third crisis in 1911 when the little nations of Serbia, Greece, Bulgaria and Montenegro on the Balkan peninsula warred among themselves. In 1913, the war in the Balkans erupted again, and again the big powers teetered on the brink.

Each new crisis was another occasion for newspaper editors to run scare headlines across the front pages. French newspapers called Germany a militarist nation bent on conquest. German newspapers talked of a ring of enemies—England on the north, France on the west, Russia on the east—conspiring to strangle Germany. Russian newspapers ridiculed the Austrians. Austrians screamed against the Serbs.

Year after year, hatreds simmered and tensions grew. To some Europeans, anticipation of war seemed worse than war itself. If it was going to happen, they were beginning to think, let it happen now before the enemy gets any stronger.

All the major powers were poised and ready for war. The only thing for which the people of Europe were unprepared was the exact nature of the crisis that would finally set the war machine in motion. Even the seven grim-faced youths in Sarajevo who waited at their separate stations along the Appel Quay with pistols and hand bombs stuffed in their pockets, didn't realize that in their hands at the moment lay the final cause for the long-dreaded war.

It was a beautiful Sunday in Sarajevo. As the crowds cheered gaily, Franz Ferdinand and Soferl rode past a bridge where a thin youth stood with a bomb in his pocket. The youth smacked one edge of the bomb against a lamp-post, pitched it at the archduke's green-plumed helmet, waited for the sharp explosion, then plunged headlong into the Miljacka River.

The bomb, however, had missed its mark. On the Appel Quay, the archduke's car had come to a stop, a safe distance from where the bomb had exploded. The archduke rose from his seat, unhurt. He inspected his wife's face and clothing. A bomb fragment had barely scratched her cheek; that was all. Had anyone in the crowd been hurt, he asked? Several had, but not seriously, and they were being taken to the hospital. Encouraging news—the assassin had been caught but had not yet confessed his motive for the crime. "Never mind, the fellow is insane," said Franz Ferdinand, and signaling the driver to start up again, he and Soferl proceeded on to Sarajevo's City Hall. There, he delivered a short speech to the joyous shouts of a crowd delirious with relief over his escape. His speech over, the archduke decided he would go to the hospital to visit those wounded by the bomb. He urged Soferl to stay behind, but she insisted on going with him. So together they climbed back into their open car and retraced their route along the Appel Quay.

Suddenly the car turned into a side street. The man sitting opposite them, an Austrian general, shouted at the driver, "What is this? This is the wrong way! We're supposed to take the Appel Quay!" At that moment, as the car braked and began to back up, someone darted out of the crowd, pistol raised, and fired two shots. Instantly, bystanders leaped on the gunman and, cursing and raging, beat him with their fists until he was senseless. Then the police came and dragged him away. In the car now racing down the Appel Quay, the archduke and Soferl stared straight ahead. For a moment the Austrian general in the car thought that by another miracle even this second assassination attempt had misfired. Then he saw blood. In his diary he recorded what happened next:

While with one hand I drew out my handkerchief to wipe the blood from the Archduke's lips, Her Highness cried, "For God's sake! What has happened to you?" Then she sank down from her seat with her face between the Archduke's knees. I had no idea that she had been hit and thought that she had fainted from shock. Then His Royal Highness said: "Soferl, Soferl! Don't die. Live for my children!" Thereupon I seized the Archduke by the coat-collar to prevent his head from sinking forwards and asked him: "Is your Royal Highness in great pain?" To which he clearly replied: "It is nothing." Now his expression changed and he repeated six or seven times: "It is nothing," more and more losing consciousness and with a fading voice.

Minutes later, Franz Ferdinand, heir to the Austrian throne, and his wife, Soferl, were dead.

Down the cobbled streets of Europe and through the outdoor cafes, rumors of the assassination passed from shop to shop and table to table. Off the German port of Kiel, the captain of the kaiser's private speedboat, overtaking the imperial yacht, flung a cigarette case at the kaiser's feet. Inside was news of the Sarajevo murder. The kaiser quickly canceled his fun at Kiel, sped back to shore and made plans to attend the archduke's funeral in Vienna.

But old Franz Josef, ruling head of Austria-Hungary, was hardened to personal tragedy by an incredible array of family disasters—the suicide of his son, the accidental death of his brother and the stabbing of his wife by a political assassin—and wished to bury his nephew Franz Ferdinand as quietly as possible. So the kaiser stayed away, and genuine mourning for the slain pair was left to the archduke's three children.

Meanwhile, in the cafes in Paris and Berlin and in the parks of London, newspaper reports of the murder at Sarajevo were read with great curiosity but little fear. It was learned that there were five other assassins in Sarajevo besides the one who missed with his bomb and the other who killed—seven assassins in all, most of them under 20 years of age. Most important of all, the assassins were Serbs and their weapons had come from Serbia, probably at the connivance of officials in the Serbian government. This was the aspect of the incident that might cause trouble. The Austrian emperor, Franz Josef, might hold Serbia responsible for the assassination of his nephew and demand drastic amends for the deed. Russia might then leap to the defense of Serbia and prepare to attack both Austria and her ally Germany simultaneously. After that there could be no stopping the dreaded war from sweeping over Europe. But it seemed at first a most unlikely chain of events, especially when Franz Josef took the loss of his nephew so calmly.

A week passed after the archduke's burial. Two weeks, and still Austria kept silent about Serbia's responsibility for the murder. Sarajevo was almost forgotten. People went back to their daily routines, and the atmosphere in European cities eased. The kaiser returned to his yachting. He expected to be sailing in the North Sea most of the summer.

Though the early weeks of July were weeks of outward calm, sensitive people felt the oncoming tragedy. In the Russian capital of St. Petersburg, at a banquet thrown by Russian Czar Nicholas II, a duchess told a French diplomat:

Do you realize that we're passing through historic days, fateful days! . . . I've had a telegram from my father today. He tells me we shall have a war before the end of the month . . . There'll be nothing left of Austria. You're going to get back Alsace and Lorraine . . . Our armies will meet in Berlin . . . Germany will be destroyed . . .

At first, such prophecies were rare, but after July 23, 1914, they were on everyone's lips. To many, it seemed as if the bodies of Franz Ferdinand and Soferl had been dug up from their graves. For on July 23, a full three and a half weeks after the murder, Austria spoke out. The Austrian government declared that Serbia must admit her responsibility for the Sarajevo murder and atone for it by submitting to 10 painfully humiliating demands, including Austrian control of investigations into the incident and censorship of all propaganda against Austria. Unless all demands were met, Austria-Hungary would declare war. Serbia had 48 hours in which to reply.

News of the Austrian ultimatum reverberated through Europe. Hearing of the ultimatum, and aware that the Russian czar was likely to go to the limit in support of Serbia, a Russian diplomat in St. Petersburg said grimly, "It is war this time."

Serbia's 48 hours passed like minutes. Along Berlin's broad, tree-lined boulevard, the Unter den Linden, thousands of solemn-faced Germans crowded outside the newspaper offices. A bulletin flashed in one of the windows: "Serbia Rejects Austrian Demands." Instantly, the crowd became a raging, chanting mob. As newspaperman Frederick Wile described it in his book, *The Assault*:

"Krieg! Krieg!" *(War! War!) it thundered.* "Nieder mit Serbien! Hoch Oesterreich!" *(Down with Serbia! Hurrah for Austria!) rang from thousands of frenzied throats. Processions formed. Men and youths, here and there women and girls, lined up, military fashion, four abreast. One cavalcade, the larger, headed toward Pariser Platz and the Brandenburg Gate. Another eastward, down the Linden. A mighty song now rent the air—"Gott erhalte Franz den Kaiser" (God save Emperor Francis), the Austrian national anthem. Then shouts yelled in the accents of imprecation—"Nieder mit Russland!" (Down with Russia!)*

In St. Petersburg, indignant crowds formed, and screamed with equal passion: "War! War! Down with Germany! Down with Austria!" Desperate to subdue the rising clamor for war, Czar Nicholas II cabled Kaiser Wilhelm:

In this most serious moment I appeal to you to help me. An ignoble war has been declared on a weak country. The indignation in Russia, shared fully by me, is enormous. I foresee that very soon I shall be overwhelmed by pressure brought upon me, and forced to take measures which will lead to war. To try and avoid such a calamity as a European war, I beg you in the name of our old friendship to do what you can to stop your allies from going too far.

The kaiser, still yachting when the crisis broke, dispatched a similar message to the czar, urgently appealing for peace. But it was not too late for the kaiser to restrain his Austrian allies. Already, Austrian soldiers were marching on the Serbian border. To protect Serbia, the czar called three million Russians to arms. The next day, the kaiser placed German troops in readiness.

As fast as their governments rushed to war, Europeans prepared to follow. French president Raymond Poincare remembered how his emotions had soared and merged with the crowd's during one stirring moment on the Champs Elysees.

As I came out of the railroad station I was greeted by an overwhelming demonstration which moved me to the depths of my being. Many people had tears in their eyes and I could hardly blink back my own. From thousands of throats arose repeated shouts of "Vive la France! Vive la Republique! Vive le President!" . . . From the station to the Elysees the cheering never stopped . . . Never have I felt so overwhelmed. Never have I found it more difficult, morally and physically, to maintain an impassive bearing. Greatness, simplicity, enthusiasm, seriousness, all combined to render this welcome unexpected, unbelievable and infinitely beautiful. Here was a united France . . .

But France was not united. The brilliant parliamentary leader of the French Socialist party, Jean Jaures, a man with a considerable following, had denounced the folly of war in his newspaper, *L'Humanite*, and urged that France stay out of any conflict that might erupt in Europe. On July 31, 1914, Jaures was killed by a single shot from a gun of a fanatic. In the street where he fell, a woman's agonized voice announced the news to the world: *"Ils ont tue Jaures!"* (They've killed Jaures!) With his death, the potential antiwar movement in France lost its spokesman and leader.

By now there was no containing the momentum toward war. The voices of people like Jaures were lost in the general clamor. A British author traveling through Russia was awakened from his sleep by the sound of running feet, shouts and alarms.

My peasant hostess cried out to me, "Have you heard the news? There is war." A young man on a fine horse came galloping down the street, a great red flag hanging from his shoulders and flapping in the wind, and as he went he called out the news to each and every one, "War! War!"

Horses out, uniforms, swords. The village feldscher (doctor's assistant) took his stand outside our one Government building . . . and began to examine horses. The Tsar had called on the Cossacks; they gave up their work without a regret and burned to fight the enemy.

It was now less than a month after the Sarajevo murder, only one week since the Austrian ultimatum. In Germany, the kaiser, home for good from a shortened summer cruise, scratched his signature on a sheet of official stationery, and Germany and Russia were at war. Tears of pride and joy rolled down the cheeks of wives and mothers in Berlin as their boys in uniform marched in perfect unison down the street, singing German hymns lustily until they were hoarse. Newspaperman Frederick Wile, visiting in Berlin at the time, described the high spirits of the marchers:

The men seemed happier than I had ever before seen German soldiers . . . The prospect of soon becoming can-

non-fodder was evidently far from depressing. Most of them carried flowers entwined round the rifle barrel or protruding from its mouth. Here and there a bouquet dangled rakishly from a helmet. Now and then a flaxen-haired Prussian girl would step into the street and press a posey into some trooper's grimy hand . . .

The German armies rapidly massed at the Belgian border, their first step in an intended drive to Paris. A few miles away, Belgian citizens thronged into the streets of Brussels to catch a glimpse of their handsome young king and cheer him on his way to parliament, where he was expected to ask for a declaration of war against Germany.

Seated inside the Belgian parliament were dignitaries from many nations, including the American ambassador, Brand Whitlock. This is Whitlock's account of the frenzied excitement of that day:

And then, while we waited, there was suddenly a noise outside, a rumble, a roar, sounds of turbulence, and then suddenly an usher shouted:
"Le Roi!" *(The King)*
And then a heavy, hoarse shout:
"Le Roi!"
The Queen, the ministers, the deputies, everybody stands . . .
"Vive le Roi! Vive le Roi! Vive le Roi!"
It is as though they could not shout it loudly enough, intensely enough, unitedly enough; they stood there, some in tears . . .

And then when the king exclaimed grandly, "The watchword is, To Arms!" the applause was thunderous, and tears streamed down every face.

That same night, in Berlin, the anger continued to mount. The British government had just announced that if Germany carried through with her threat to invade Belgium, England would join France and Russia in the war. A large crowd of Germans formed outside the British embassy in Berlin and heaved stones at embassy windows, shouting loudly with every sound of shattering glass. In

London, another crowd was gathering outside the British Parliament, gazing anxiously upward at the hands of Big Ben. At midnight, unless some miracle happened, England would go to war against Germany.

In an office close by, the young First Lord of the Admiralty, Winston Churchill, then in command of the British Navy, sat quietly by himself while the last minutes of peace ticked slowly away. Later he remembered the strange atmosphere of those minutes:

War would be declared at midnight. As far as we had been able to foresee the event, all our preparations were made. Mobilisation was complete. Every ship was in its station; every man at his post. All over the world, every British captain and admiral was on guard. It only remained to give the signal . . . In the War Room of the Admiralty, where I sat waiting, one could hear the clock tick. From Parliament Street came the murmurs of the crowd; but they sounded distant and the world seemed very still. The tumult of the struggle for life was over: it was succeeded by the silence of ruin and death.

For a short time after the midnight hours struck, the English were the last people—following the Austrians, the Serbs, the Russians, the Germans, the French and the Belgians—to be trapped in the chain of madness set in motion by a young Serb's hatred for an Austrian archduke. Before the madness ended, however, it was fated to spread around the world.

3

THANK GOD
FOR THE ATLANTIC

GERMANY DECLARES WAR ON RUSSIA, FIRST
SHOTS ARE FIRED: the headline stretched across the top
of the *New York Times* on August 2, 1914. Repeated in
different forms in newspapers all over the country, its
alarming message turned what would have been a typical
Sunday into a gloomy day across the United States. The
Times editorial attempted to put the nation's shock and
horror into words:

> *With Germany's declaration of war against Russia, the*
> *bloodiest war ever fought on earth and the least justified*
> *of all wars since man emerged from barbarism has appar-*
> *ently begun . . .*
> *The threat of war on this unprecedented scale, its very*
> *nearness, the overwhelming fear that it may not be averted*
> *are proofs of the backwardness of Europe. By permitting*
> *themselves to be brought so near to war they prove that*
> *their civilization is half a sham. They have reverted to the*
> *condition of savage tribes roaming the forests and falling*
> *upon each other in a fury of blood and carnage to achieve*
> *the ambitious designs of chieftains clad in skins and drunk*
> *with mead.*

Americans felt lucky that day that they lived far away from Europe and its prospect of "blood and carnage." As millions of German, Russian and English boys prepared to kill each other in a senseless war, American boys faced nothing more serious than the opening of school in the fall. The Atlantic Ocean, or "Great Pond" as some called it, had served in the past to keep the United States safely removed from European wars. So long as the Atlantic did not evaporate, there was little reason to fear that Americans would be drawn into this war either.

At least, that was the view of the average citizen. And as the war began in August 1914, it was also the view of American politicians and leaders, including President Woodrow Wilson. In the White House, Wilson received lengthy letters and telegrams from American ambassadors in the various capitals of Europe. From London came this message by ambassador Walter H. Page about the turbulent first days of war:

All London has been awake for a week. Soldiers are marching day and night; immense throngs block the streets about the government offices. But they are all very orderly. Every day Germans are arrested on suspicion; and several of them have committed suicide. Yesterday one poor American woman yielded to the excitement and cut her throat. I find it hard to get about much. People stop me on the street, follow me to luncheon, grab me as I come out of any committee meeting—to know my opinion of this or that—how can they get home? Will such-and-such a boat fly the American flag? . . . I have to fight my way about and rush to an automobile . . . I have not had a bath for three days; as soon as I get in the tub, the telephone [rings] an "urgent" call!

In closing, Page remembered to give thanks for the great sea that separated the United States from the scene of the impending war:

. . . I thank heaven for many things—first, the Atlantic Ocean . . . Now, when all this half of the world will suffer the unspeakable brutalization of war, we shall preserve our moral strength, our political powers, and our ideals.

God save us!

President Wilson's distress about Page's report and other accounts of the events in Europe was compounded by a terrible personal crisis. In the White House, his wife lay dying from Bright's disease. On August 6, the president and his three daughters gathered around Ellen Wilson's bedside for the last time. When the doctor's solemn nod announced her death, the Wilson girls, Eleanor, Jessica and Margaret, for the first time in their memory, saw their father weep openly. Now, without his wife's counsel and support, the president had to face the European crisis alone.

Turning to his responsibilities as president, Wilson had every intention of keeping the United States out of the European war. He recognized, however, that the task would not be easy. For one thing, he feared that the sympathies of the American people—and especially the feelings of the foreign-born—might begin to favor one side in the war. If that happened, then U.S. policy toward the warring nations might also tilt in one direction rather than remaining strictly neutral.

Of course, immigrants recently arrived from Russia, Germany or Austria had strong feelings about the side they favored. The majority of Americans, however, had lost most of their Old World ties. Perhaps if they could be made to see that it was urgent, they would remain impartial and enable the United States, as a truly neutral nation, to avoid becoming embroiled in the war. This at least was President Wilson's hope when, on August 19, he concluded a newspaper message to the American people in these words:

I venture, therefore, my fellow countrymen, to speak a solemn word of warning to you against that deepest, most subtle, most essential breach of neutrality which may spring out of partisanship, out of passionately taking sides. The United States must be neutral in fact as well as in name during these days that are to try men's souls . . .

Even as President Wilson made this appeal, however, news reports gave Americans the distinct impression that

Germany was more to blame for the coming of war than any of its foes. Many Americans thought Germany acted monstrously in the first week of war by invading the little nation of Belgium. Out of Belgium came grim stories of the wholesale murder of women and children by German troops. The Belgian government issued a long official report substantiating some of these rumors.

The day of August 23 was made bloody by several more massacres. German soldiers discovered some inhabitants of the Faubourg St. Pierre in the cellars of a brewery there and shot them.

Since the previous evening a crowd of workmen belonging to the factory of M. Himmer had hidden themselves, along with their wives and children, in the cellars of the building. They had been joined there by many neighbours and several members of the family of their employer. About six o'clock in the evening these unhappy people made up their minds to come out of their refuge, and defiled, all trembling from the cellars with the white flag in front. They were immediately seized and violently attacked by the soldiers. Every man was shot on the spot. Almost all the men of the Faubourg de Neffe were executed en masse. In another part of the town twelve civilians were killed in a cellar. In the Rue en Ile a paralytic was shot in his arm-chair. In the Rue Enfer the soldiers killed a young boy of fourteen.

In the Faubourg de Neffe the viaduct of the railway was the scene of a bloody massacre. An old woman and all her children were killed in their cellar. A man of sixty-five years and his wife, his son, and his daughter were shot against a wall. Other inhabitants of Neffe were taken in a barge as far as the rock of Bayard and shot there, among them a woman of eighty-three and her husband.

After many such accounts, the American newspaper-reading public no longer objected when cartoonists pictured Kaiser Wilhelm and his soldiers as uncivilized brutes, their jaws dripping blood.

To be sure, there were skeptical Americans who scoffed at the tales of atrocity coming out of Belgium. Others,

mostly Americans of German origin, wrote indignant letters to their newspapers accusing them of spreading "ma-
licious falsehoods." In a letter to the editor of the *New York
Herald,* one German-American pleaded: "All I ask is, be
fair, give the Germans a square deal. More we do not
desire." But this appeal and thousands like it were ig-
nored.

Even when newspapers reported events with strict ac-
curacy, however, Germany's reputation in America continued to fall. It was generally known that the German army
had systematically and deliberately destroyed the Belgian
town of Louvain in order to punish the people for the
killing of one of its soldiers by a Belgian sniper and that
German officials, far from apologizing, had boasted of the
deed. And it was indisputable that thousands of Belgians,
driven from their homes and farms, had been forced to flee
in terror before the advancing German army. Richard
Harding Davis, an American war correspondent, described the entrance of these fugitives into Brussels,
Belgium's capital city.

*The voices of the cars racing past were like the voices
of human beings driven with fear. From the front of the
hotel we watched them. There were taxicabs, racing cars,
limousines. They were crowded with women and children of the rich, and of the nobility and gentry from the
great chateaux far to the west. Those who occupied them
were white-faced with the dust of the road, with weari-
ness and fear. In cars magnificently upholstered, padded
and cushioned were piled trunks, hand-bags, dressing-
cases. The women had dressed at a moment's warning,
as though at a cry of fire. Many had traveled throughout
the night, and in their arms the children, snatched from
the pillows, were sleeping.*

A simple photograph of the German army in dress
parade expressed as well as anything Germany's growing
reputation for ruthlessness. To Brand Whitlock, the American ambassador to Belgium, the German soldiers in their
heavy spiked helmets and tall black boots looked like a
gigantic, all-powerful machine as they goose-stepped into

Brussels. The sound of their slapping boots and rumbling cannon wheels continued to oppress his spirits through the day and far into the night. He described the effect in his diary:

It became monstrous, oppressive, unendurable: monstrous, somehow, those black guns on grey carriages and grey caissons; and those grey uniforms, the insolent faces of those supercilious young officers—scarred in their silly duels—wearing monocles; those dull plodding soldiers—such backs, such thews and sinews, the heels of their stout, heavy boots beating on the pavement; as impressive as a spectacle—all the attention to detail that distinguishes a circus in America; but in its implications, horrible, appalling, dreadful.

Tireless as a machine, the German army didn't rest in Brussels but pressed relentlessly forward, crossing the Belgian border into northern France. There it occupied French villages and kicked the French and British forces aside like so many autumn leaves. Another two days' march and Paris might have fallen like Brussels. But then, at the last minute, the French stopped the Germans and even pushed them back a few miles. The French and British thanked God for their deliverance.

And so did most Americans. After following the European war for only a month, they well understood what *Life* magazine meant when, in an editorial of September 1914 it called Germany "the bully of Europe."

No doubt in our character as neutrals we ought to be as sorry as we can for everybody involved in the great war, without stopping to be over-nice in apportioning blame . . .

And coming to particulars, we ought especially to be sorry for the Germans. As we see them to-day they are a pathetic people. Germany has set up to be the bully of Europe, and a bully, when one has got over being mad at him is always pathetic. Bullies are always stupid . . . They are people who, seeing no chance to get what they want by favour are constantly tempted to try to get what they want by force.

1914

Germany characterized by the American artist
Boardman Robinson as a murderous brute in spiked
helmet. (Credit: New York Public Library)

That seems to be the case with the Germans . . . In his present stage of development, the German is the fat man of Europe whom nobody loves.

After all the negative publicity about Germany, most Americans found it difficult to heed Wilson's warning against "that deepest, most subtle, most essential breach of neutrality, which may spring out of partisanship, out of passionately taking sides." Entering the new year, 1915, Americans were neutral in fact but not in spirit. They believed they could freely sympathize with Belgium and condemn Germany and still remain safely at peace across the protective waters of the Atlantic. Few, therefore, were as alarmed as President Wilson by the following notice which appeared in the *New York Times* on February 5, 1915, under the headline GERMANY PROCLAIMS WAR ZONE:

The waters around Great Britain and Ireland, including the whole English Channel are declared a war zone from and after Feb. 18, 1915.
Every merchant ship found in this war zone will be destroyed, even if it is impossible to avert dangers which threaten crew and passengers.
Also neutral ships in the war zone are in danger . . .

Though most people dismissed this threat as a desperate and preposterous move on Germany's part, not to be taken seriously, President Wilson immediately called a cabinet meeting. Whether Americans realized it or not, their sons' lives were on the line.

4

WARNING!

Albert J. Beveridge, journalist and one-time senator from Indiana, knew more about the German war zone than most Americans and even most Germans. He had the inside story. Days before anyone had heard of the new war zone, he had interviewed the man most responsible for the policy, Grand Admiral von Tirpitz, commander of the German fleet. He had found the admiral in his temporary but elegant wartime headquarters, a wealthy Frenchman's house confiscated by the German armies during their advance through eastern France.

In the interview, Tirpitz inquired what it was that had turned American public opinion so strongly against Germany. When Beveridge explained that Americans considered Germany a militaristic nation, glorying in war, Tirpitz called the notion "monstrous," "foolish," "idiotic." The British were the real warmongers, he said, not Germany. Then, probing for a reaction to a rumor he had heard, Beveridge remarked slyly:

"It has been said, Your Excellency, that you have suggested a submarine blockade of England."

"Well, why not?" came like a shot from a big gun. "Why not, I say? England is trying to starve us. She could not do that if we did not get a pound of provisions from other countries! But she is trying to do so. Are we not to retaliate?

Why is it that whatever England does seems all right to Americans, while they object to anything Germany does, of the same kind?"

Tirpitz had a point. Almost immediately after the outbreak of the war, the British navy had blockaded German ports, stopping merchant ships bound for Germany and seizing their cargo. What was the difference, the admiral asked Beveridge, between a British blockade and a German blockade?

Beveridge knew the answer and so did Tirpitz: the submarine. Unable to blockade British waters from her inferior geographical position with a small surface fleet, Germany had recently begun to rely upon a weapon new to warfare, the Untersee (undersea) boat, or submarine. Underwater, the U-boat was a deadly craft; above water, however, it was helpless and vulnerable. It could not afford to wait for passengers and crew to climb safely into lifeboats before firing. If it was to sink a merchant ship, a submarine had to strike without warning. Beveridge reminded Tirpitz:

"But a submarine blockade is not the same as an ordinary blockade, where merchant ships can be warned before sinking . . . a submarine blockade gives the blockade runner no chance."

"But what chance does a mine give the merchant ship?" quickly exclaimed Germany's master sailor. *"It gives less chance even than a submarine. If we decide upon a submarine blockade of England, we shall notify the world. Yet England has sowed the North Sea and the Channel with mines, so as to shut us from the ocean and keep supplies away from us. These hundreds of mines give no warning."*

Beveridge said he had heard that Germany also planted mines in the North Sea.

"Another gigantic English lie!" exclaimed the German admiral. He continued:

"It is astonishing that you Americans, the shrewdest people in the world, should credit England's statement that

we Germans do everything that is foolish and wicked, and nothing that is sensible and good! . . ."

"But, Your Excellency, we are neutral; we wish to be impartial and just, even in thought, as our President has said," I remarked.

"Neutral!" exclaimed this builder of Germany's sea power. "When you are sending provisions to England, France, Russia—and none to us! Neutral! When you are supplying our enemies with rifles, guns, ammunition—and selling none to us! Tell me"—and this mighty figure of a man rose to his feet, towering like an ancient viking, whose picture he resembles—"do you call that neutral?"

There was some truth to Tirpitz's charges. For while the United States had accepted the planting of mines in the North Sea by the British without protest, she later charged Germany with inhumane warfare for her use of the submarine. And Beveridge could not deny that the United States had been shipping munitions wholesale to the Allied nations.

Shortly after the interview with Tirpitz, Beveridge received the news that Germany was officially announcing a war zone, or submarine blockade. It came as no surprise.

To President Wilson, however, the news was like a prophecy of doom. The president knew that the submarine issue could draw the United States into the war. To prevent this from happening, he could do one of two things. Heeding Germany's warning, he could prohibit Americans from sailing into the war zone—but this would violate America's traditional and cherished right to freedom on the high seas. Or he could try to make Germany abandon her submarine campaign by issuing a warning of his own.

For five days, Wilson wrestled with the problem. Then, on February 10, he sent a note to the German government. The message was as strongly worded as diplomatic language would allow. It denied the legitimacy of the German war zone and affirmed the United States' lawful rights to trade and travel. If these rights were violated by German submarines, Wilson's note warned, Germany would be held to "a strict accountability."

Wilson had deep misgivings about this message. He wondered if the words "strict accountability" were too weak. If so, the message would do no good. But if they were too strong, it would be just as bad, for then his fellow countrymen might expect him to declare war if ever a German U-boat, by accident or design, took an American life.

The warning almost worked. The words Wilson was worried about, "strict accountability," did sound all too strong and warlike to Germany's excitable chancellor Bethmann-Hollweg, who pleaded with the kaiser to modify his war zone decree. Accordingly, over the indignant protests of Grand Admiral von Tirpitz the kaiser ordered all U-boat commanders to take the strictest precautions against sinking American ships.

Unfortunately, this change in policy only played into the hands of Great Britain. It was all too easy for the captains of British merchant ships to fly the American flag whenever they entered submarine waters. And if the United States objected to the misuse of her flag, Britain had a ready answer. When it was discovered that the *Lusitania*, Britain's largest and most luxurious passenger liner, had flown the American flag on a recent voyage, the ship's owner justified the action with some shrewd logic:

Remember that the Lusitania *carried a number of American citizens and a large amount of American property. It was the captain's business to get them safely to port. Let the Germans ask the Americans if they would drown rather than get to port on a British ship flying the American flag. You can safely leave the answer to the Americans. They know.*

The ruse worked, however, only so long as Germany stood for it. Then the inevitable happened. When a German U-boat, acting under instruction to respect the American flag, was treacherously rammed and sunk by a British merchant ship, the kaiser lost his patience. Now Grand Admiral von Tirpitz had his way again. All restrictions on U-boat commanders were lifted; they were to sink anything that sailed into the war zone.

One commander was especially pleased to receive his new instructions. Young, blond Captain Walter Schwieger had long chafed under a policy that limited his U-20's effectiveness. At last he would be free to sink vessels without first having to identify their flags. Schwieger's new orders read:

Large English troop transports expected starting from Liverpool, Bristol Channel, Dartmouth. In order to do considerable damage to transports, U-20 and U-27 are dispatched as soon as possible. Assign stations there. Get to stations on the fastest possible route around Scotland; hold them as long as supplies permit. U-30 has orders to go to Dartmouth. Submarines are to attack transport ships, merchant ships, warships. Wire time of departure.

On April 30, 1915, Captain Schwieger wired that the U-20 under his command was leaving Germany that day for the waters off Liverpool. That same day, 3,000 miles away in New York City, the crew of the British merchant ship *Lusitania* was preparing the magnificent liner for another Atlantic crossing. She was to sail at noon, May 1, 1915, and dock at Liverpool in one week.

For the *Lusitania's* passengers in New York, the first day of May 1915 began with a flurry of activity. Children had to be dressed in their best traveling clothes. Suitcases and handbags needed checking. Last-minute phone calls to friends and relatives had to be made. All this done, the travelers left their apartments or checked out of their New York hotels, taxied over to the Cunard Line's gigantic pier and finally joined the crowd of strangers waving merrily from the decks of the great ship.

Although the passengers were mainly British, the list included over 200 Americans, most of them heading for Europe on business. Among these was Alfred Vanderbilt, one of America's wealthiest men, on his way to England to watch one of his horses race in the London derby. He had stubbornly insisted on going despite an excited phone call from his mother warning him of a small bulletin in the morning's paper:

NOTICE!

TRAVELLERS *intending to embark on the Atlantic voyage are reminded that a state of war exists between Germany and her allies and Great Britain and her allies; that the zone of war includes the waters adjacent to the British Isles; that, in accordance with formal notice given by the Imperial Government, vessels flying the flag of Great Britain, or of any of her allies, are liable to destruction in those waters and that travellers sailing in the war zone on ships of Great Britain or her allies do so at their own risk.*

IMPERIAL GERMAN EMBASSY
Washington, D.C., April 22, 1915

Alfred Vanderbilt laughed at the German warning. "Well, how ridiculous this thing is," he scoffed to reporters. "The Germans would not dare to make any attempt to sink the ship."

On the track of a good story, newspaper reporters asked other passengers for their reactions to the German warning. Almost everybody agreed that there was no danger since they were assured by an agent of the Cunard Line that a ship as fast as the Lusitania could easily elude slow-moving submarines and their torpedoes. "As for submarines," said the Cunard representative, "I have no fear of them whatever."

So, dismissing the German warning from their minds, almost 2,000 passengers and crew breathed the fresh sea air and watched the New York skyline slowly fade into the distance. Ahead lay seven luxurious days at sea.

Six days passed uneventfully. Off the west coast of England, a German U-boat bobbed on an empty sea. So far, Captain Schwieger had done no better under the new instructions than under the old. Now he was running low on both fuel and torpedoes. He would have to head for home. But perhaps on the way his luck would turn. Schwieger wrote in his diary:

May 6—Only three torpedoes are still available. I wish to save two, if possible, for the return trip. It is therefore decided to remain south of the entrance into the Bristol

Channel and to attack steamers until two-fifths of the fuel oil has been used up, especially since chances for favorable attacks are better here and enemy defensive measures less effective, than in the Irish Sea near Liverpool.

The next morning, passengers crowded the rail on the *Lusitania's* port side: Ireland. A little later, turning their backs on the green shoreline, they filed into the ship's great dining room for the last luncheon of the voyage.

As they ate, Captain Schwieger, in the conning tower of his submarine, raised his binoculars and scanned the horizon. Suddenly he stopped short and focused on a point in the distance. Later he recorded in his log the dramatic events that followed:

Ahead and to starboard four funnels and two masts of a steamer with course perpendicular to us come into sight . . . Ship is made out to be a large passenger steamer. We submerged to a depth of eleven meters and went ahead at full speed, taking a course converging with the one of the steamers hoping it might change its course to starboard, along the Irish coast. The steamer turns to starboard, takes course to Queenstown, thus making possible an approach for a shot. Until 3 P.M. we ran at high speed in order to gain position directly ahead. Clean bow shot from 700 meters range . . .

On board the *Lusitania*, a man from St. Louis was sitting in the ship's saloon. He recalled later:

We had been playing poker ever since the trip began, and someone had just ordered a round of beer. As we started to drink, one of the fellows said: "What would you do if a torpedo hit us?" I said: "I am unmarried, and I'd finish my beer."

At that moment, the torpedo struck.

. . . the others bolted, but I finished the beer and went over to the bar and called for another bottle and said to the bartender: "Let's die game, anyway." But he said:

"You go to hell" and bolted, leaving me all alone. I had another drink, and just as I was finishing it the boat turned over.

Robert Rankin of Washington, D.C., was walking the deck trying to digest his meal.

We saw what looked like a whale or a porpoise [he wrote] rising about three-quarters of a mile to starboard. We all knew what it was, but no one named it. It came straight for the ship. It was obvious it couldn't miss. It was aimed ahead of her and struck under the bridge. I saw it disappear. We all hoped for the fraction of a second it would not explode. But the explosion came clear up through the upper deck, and pieces of the wreckage fell clean aft of where we were standing. We ducked into the smoking-room for shelter from the flying debris.

At first there was little panic on board. The captain assured the passengers that the ship was not seriously damaged and instructed the crew not to lower the lifeboats. Minutes later, a shuddering explosion threw people to the deck. Then the panic began. Women's screams, children's sobs, men's curses filled the air.

For Captain Schwieger, the last minutes of the *Lusitania* made an unforgettable sight.

The ship stops immediately and quickly heels to starboard, at the same time diving deeper at the bows. She has the appearance of being about to capsize. Great confusion on board, boats being cleared and part being lowered to water. They must have lost their heads. Many boats crowded come down head first or stern first, in the water, and immediately fill and sink.

Fewer lifeboats can be made clear on the port side, owing to the slant of the ship. The ship blows off. In the front appears the name Lusitania in gold letters . . . It seems as if the vessel will be afloat only a short time. Submerge to twenty-four meters and go to sea. I could not have fired a second torpedo into this throng of humanity attempting to save themselves.

Now the chilling sea swirled with bodies and wreckage. In a badly damaged lifeboat, a young doctor from South Dakota struggled for his life.

We pushed away hard to avoid the suck, but our boat was filling and we bailed fast with one bucket and the women's hats. The man with the bucket became exhausted and I relieved him. In a few minutes she was filled level full. Then a keg floated up and I pitched it about ten feet away and followed it. After reaching it I turned to see the fate of our boat. She had capsized and covered many . . .

At the scene of the catastrophe the surface of the water seemed dotted with bodies. Only a few of the lifeboats seemed to be doing any good. The cries of "My God!" "Save us!" and "Help!" gradually grew weaker from all sides and finally a low weeping, wailing, inarticulate sound, mingled with coughing and gurgling, made me heartsick. I saw many men die . . .

The number of passengers and crew who drowned in the cold Atlantic water on May 7, 1915, was 1,198. Among the dead were 128 Americans (most famous of whom was the millionaire, Alfred Vanderbilt).

In the United States that evening, President Wilson was just finishing dinner when someone came in with a telegram:

LUSITANIA SUNK AT 2:30. PROBABLY MANY SURVIVORS. RESCUE WORK PROGRESSING FAVORABLY.

Wilson immediately rose and, without a word to anyone, went out for a walk. He refused to answer reporters' questions about how he meant to respond to the tragedy.

Reporters had no better luck talking with the German ambassador to the United States, Count Von Bernstorff. It was Bernstorff who had issued the warning notice about the *Lusitania* sailing. Now reporters taunted him with questions:

"Don't you think it's up to you to make some statement?" . . .

"I shall not say one word. Not one word. Not one word."
"Do you think the sinking of the Lusitania *was justifiable?"* . . .
"I said that I would not say a word. Not one word."
"Yes, but don't you believe this is cold-blooded murder?"
. . . *but there was no answer, and he hurried into a telephone booth.*

Bernstorff knew that it was pointless to argue. Except for his German-American friends, no one in America would listen to Germany's case. His government had given fair warning; he had repeated that warning, but it had done no good. Americans would never blame themselves or the British navy for what had happened. When they read newspaper reports like the following, they thought only of a fiendish kaiser, a merciless Grand Admiral von Tirpitz, and a cruel and so-far nameless captain of a German U-boat:

CORK, IRELAND—*On the Cunard wharf lies a mother with a three months old child clasped tightly in her arms. Her face wears a half smile. Her baby's head rests against her breast. No one has tried to separate them. Several other babies have been found, whom no one has yet identified. Two children's bodies—little girls—were recovered. They are clasped in each other's arms.*

Across the nation, newspapers printed sermons and other statements about the disaster. Bringing to mind the gray faces of the drowned, a New York minister reflected the change in many people's attitudes toward the war when he shouted from his pulpit:

This sinking of the Cunarder is not war; it is murder! It is not piracy, for piracy has no Government behind it. This is organized murder and no language is too strong to call it. It is the Black Hole of Calcutta, the Massacre of St. Bartholomew and the Piracy of the Barbary Coast rolled into one. It is on a level of poison in wells. I call it murder most foul . . .
The situation is getting too hard for individuals. If I see a ruffian in the street beating a boy I may want to be

neutral. I may say I know neither ruffian nor boy. But God help me; I am less than a man if I don't thrust in my hand. It is too much to ask me to keep out. So it is getting to be too much to ask America to keep out when Americans are drowned as part of a European war.

On all sides, Americans braced themselves for war. Most were ready to fight as soon as President Wilson gave the call. Many believed it was the only honorable thing to do. Remembering the phrase "strict accountability," they waited for the president to follow up his words with deeds.

For three days they waited. All this time, Wilson said nothing, saw no one. Finally he emerged from his White House study and boarded a train for Philadelphia, where he was scheduled to address a group of immigrants. As the mayor of Philadelphia introduced the speaker of the day, "I present to you—God bless him—the President," the auditorium rocked with ecstatic, patriotic cheering. There was little question of the people's readiness for war. Wherever the president led them, they would follow. They listened impatiently for a sign of his intentions. Finally it came:

The example of America must be a special example. The example of America must be the example not merely of peace because it will not fight, but of peace because peace is the healing and elevating influence of the world and strife is not. There is such a thing as a nation being so right that it does not need to convince others by force that it is right.

The next day, the morning's headline in the *New York Times* proclaimed: PRESIDENT'S PLEA IS STILL FOR PEACE.

5

THREE MEN, A WOMAN AND A STUDENT

So it was to be peace after all—but such an indefinite, fragile peace that no one could tell how long it would last. A full month passed after the sinking of the *Lusitania* and then an entire summer, and still people wondered if the United States might yet enter the war against Germany. Any American who happened to be in France or England in the spring and summer of 1915 was besieged with anxious questions. Marie Van Vorst, an American woman helping to care for French soldiers in a Red Cross hospital in Paris, wrote to a friend back home:

Of course they asked themselves and me every minute what America was going to do, and one was pretty safe in feeling that the first question a person would put to you when they met you was just that: "What is America going to do?" I'll be switched if I could tell them or make any kind of a satisfactory answer. It is all too dulling and strange . . .

The situation was dulling and strange to more Americans than Marie Van Vorst. Before the *Lusitania*, America had seemed safely removed from the European war. Now, suddenly, that sense of remoteness and perfect security was gone and it was hard to see what could restore it. On

September 1, 1915, however, the tension was eased slightly when the German government, speaking through its ambassador, Count von Bernstorff, expressed regret for the drowning of 128 Americans aboard the *Lusitania* and two others on another torpedoed British ship. Bernstorff promised there would be no more such accidents. "Liners will not be sunk by our submarines," he pledged, "without warning and without safety of the lives of noncombatants, provided that the liners do not try to escape or offer resistance." But Germany might be false to her word. Or the captain of a German submarine, impatient for a kill at sea, might violate his instructions. After the *Lusitania*, anything could happen to plunge America into war.

Strangest of all, Americans no longer knew whether getting involved in the war was morally right or wrong. True commitment on the question was rare. Among the few who took a strong vocal stand were, on the one side, Red Cross nurse Marie Van Vorst, an ex-president, Theodore Roosevelt, and a high-minded student from Princeton University, Archie Taber, and on the other, a band of idealists and humanitarians—including Socialist leader Eugene V. Debs and Democratic statesman William Jennings Bryan. These three men, a woman and a student were among the few who acted vigorously for their beliefs, making speeches and writing letters and articles and even volunteering to go to France, while the majority of Americans sat and listened and shrugged their shoulders, or believed one thing one day, another thing the next.

Red Cross nurse Marie Van Vorst was disturbed to see her countrymen in this uncertain state of mind because she, at least, believed she knew exactly what they must do. She wished they could hear for themselves the talk of German brutality that one heard every day on the streets of Paris and London. Then they would understand why America belonged heart and soul in the war. "Children have been thrown on the flames of burning houses," she said in one letter. "Women with child have been slaughtered before the eyes of the inhabitants." She wrote a letter to the *New York Sun* in which she quoted words alleged to be the kaiser's orders to his troops: "When you meet the foe, you will defeat him. No quarter will be given, no prisoners taken. Let all who fall into your hands be at your mercy. Gain a reputation like the Huns under Attila." The German soldiers carried out the kaiser's orders with a vengeance, Marie Van Vorst affirmed, and she therefore followed the French and English practice of calling them "Huns."

The savagery of "the Hun" was one of Marie Van Vorst's reasons for wanting America in the war. Also, participation would give a much needed lift to America's national spirit. The war, she wrote, "should not only try men's souls but make men's souls." She had seen it happen. In the Red Cross hospitals in Paris, she had seen torn and mutilated French soldiers bear the agony of their wounds in silence and prepare for death uncomplaining, knowing that they died in a noble cause. She marveled at the women in the hospitals who worked without rest amidst the hideous stench of wounded and rotting flesh.

Throughout France, the war had awakened a spirit of service and gallantry. A French count, a friend of Marie Van Vorst, sensed one night the certainty of his own death, and wrote this message just before going into his last battle:

I offer with all my heart to God the sacrifice of my life for my beloved country and for the protection of those I love, in order to repair by my personal sacrifice any ill I may ever have done to my neighbor. I thank without ceasing every one who has ever been good to me; I pray for them in going, and I in turn beseech them to pray for me.

War, though ghastly to think about, had its redeeming features for Marie Van Vorst and other American women working in hospitals overseas. It brought out the manhood and nobility in a boy. In this sense, the United States, by staying out of the fight, was denying her young men a chance to develop that grandeur of spirit that a Red Cross nurse witnessed every day in the patient suffering of wounded Frenchmen.

In 1915, the only chance a young American had to test his courage in the war under his own flag was as a volunteer in the American Field Ambulance, a privately sponsored organization engaged in rescuing wounded Frenchmen from the battlefield. Ambulance drivers were known to have been killed by German artillery fire on their dash back to the Paris hospitals. This prospect of doing a good deed under dangerous conditions set America's college youth to thinking about quitting school just to see a bit of the war in the American Field Ambulance. Those who finally decided on going were much alike. Physically they were hearty, vigorous, athletic. They were crazy about such things as automobiles and the outdoor life. They believed their mission in life was to serve humanity. In short, they were youths like Archie Taber, a volunteer from Princeton University.

Archie's full name was Arthur Richmond Taber. In naming him Arthur, his parents had though of the high-minded English king whom legend depicted at a round table surrounded by noble, strong-armed knights. When he was an infant, Archie's blond curls and lace dresses looked girlish, but they fooled no one. Archie was going to be a man among men. His mother would see to that. Once when she and Archie were away for the summer she wrote to Mr. Taber about the kinds of things she expected of Archie even as a three-year-old. "I keep impressing upon him that he must be stronger, braver and kinder too . . . and I have begun to talk to him about his being master over his little body."

At the age of eight, Archie had become everything his parents wanted. In 1901, Mrs. Taber wrote in a letter:

Arthur is ruggedness personified. He not only bathed in our ice-cold lake for one-half hour . . . and came home warm and well, but he is now sleeping out on the back porch every night, without a soul at hand—a triumph of courage, I think. We have dreadful thunderstorms but he says he can't get wet there, and that if a burglar tries to get into the house that way, he'll be there to catch him! So I'm quite proud of my small man.

Still the lessons in manliness continued. At ten, according to another letter written by his mother, Archie concluded his evening prayers with "Make me honourable, truthful, clean, kind and brave." As a teenager, he was high-spirited, strong, handsome, courageous. When a snake bit him one day and a friend said he didn't know whether it was a copperhead or a rattlesnake, he didn't flinch. He underwent nine painful operations for a wrenched knee without complaint. He was constantly looking for ways to test his fortitude. Once he nearly died trying to find out how long he could survive alone without water, in a Western desert. It was as if Archie had been training since birth to risk his life before German artillery fire, rushing to the aid of wounded soldiers in France. No one who knew him, therefore, was in the least surprised when he said he was leaving Princeton to join the American Field Ambulance. In a letter to his mother, a relative wrote: "It is wonderful that Archie is starting out on so heroic a mission . . . I think he leads a charmed life anyway." So Archie Taber, eager to involve himself in the war though his country held back, shook hands with his father, kissed his mother good-bye and sailed for France.

By far the most famous supporter of the war was a rugged, rough-and-tumble American who liked to wear cowboy hats and African safari helmets. Boys like Archie Taber devoured the books he wrote about his adventures in the wild. The American people called him affectionately "the Colonel," "T.R." and "Teddy," because his full name, Theodore Roosevelt, seemed too stuffy for the kind of man he was. The Colonel was the very picture of manliness, patriotism and success. Between 1901 and 1909 he had been president of the United States and had turned a part of the White House into a gym so that he could take his daily exercise wrestling. He liked to close his day by taking on his four young sons in a pillow fight. On speakers' platforms campaigning for election he would gnash his teeth and clench his fists as if he were still wrestling, and whenever he could, he sought an opportunity to display his physical courage and stamina. He still longed to recapture that glorious moment when, three years before his presidency, he had led a cavalry charge up San Juan Hill in Cuba and had a hand in winning the Spanish-American War. At that time, he had resigned his job as assistant secretary of the Navy to organize and lead a regiment of volunteers called the Rough Riders. His charge up San Juan Hill so impressed the schoolboys of the time that they wore Rough Rider outfits and planned to be like the Colonel when they grew up.

In 1915, the Colonel was fifty-six years old, but he refused to accept the possibility that his most glorious days were behind him. Should the United States declare war, he had a plan for organizing a whole division of troops that he personally would lead to France. As he described his plan to an army friend:

My hope is, if we are drawn into the European war, to get Congress to authorize me to raise a Cavalry Division, which would consist of four cavalry brigades each of two regiments, and a brigade of Horse Artillery of two regiments, with a pioneer battalion of signal troops in addition to a supply train and a sanitary train. I would wish the ammunition train and the supply train to be both motor trains; and I would also like a regiment or battalion of machine guns . . .

The only thing that interfered with the Colonel's plan was Woodrow Wilson. Roosevelt, a Republican, had long disliked Wilson because Wilson was a Democrat. Now, in 1915, he despised him. He thought Wilson a coward for not taking America to war over the *Lusitania*.

To the Colonel, Wilson with his long, gaunt, bespectacled face both looked and acted like a weakling. "Wilson is a physically timid man," he said in a letter. "He is anxious to avoid war at all hazards. He is an entirely cold-blooded, self-seeking man." And the American people were no better, he charged in letters, speeches and magazine articles, if they said and did nothing while Germany butchered innocent women and children. He toured the country, shaking his fists at great audiences from New York to San Francisco to let them know that he was disappointed with them for putting up with Wilson's weakling policy.

At first, attitudes like Roosevelt's had little impact on the basic indecision of the American people, but eventually they began to penetrate to the national conscience and sense of honor. As 1915 passed into 1916, Wilson's policy of neutrality sounded ever more hollow and ineffectual. Despite Germany's pledge to hold her submarines in check, 14 Americans aboard an Italian liner, the *Ancona*, were drowned at sea from the attack of an Austrian submarine, and two others died aboard the *Persia*. Wilson's practice of sending diplomatic notes of protest to Germany following every incident became something of an international joke. The Colonel treated it as a scandal. In Detroit, he made this shocking pronouncement:

We have suffered as a nation from prolonged and excessive indulgence in notewriting . . . As a matter of fact, while we have been writing these notes, the loss of life among non-combatant men, women and children on the ships which were torpedoed and about which we wrote notes, has exceeded the total number of lives lost in both the Union and Confederate Navies during the entire Civil War. Think of that, friends!

But if the Colonel's arguments for war were strong, so too were Eugene V. Debs's arguments for peace. Gene Debs was a lean fellow with a bald head whom people knew by the gentle look in his eyes to be an honest man but whom the newspapers said had once served time in jail. It was a common thing, in the 1890s when Debs was a young man, to go to jail for leading railroad workers out on strike, and in 1894 that's what Debs had done. But Gene Debs was an honest man, as honest as T.R. or Archie Taber, and as manly too. As a teenager, he had taken a job stoking coal into railroad engines and worked his thin, sinewy body until it was blistered and raw. He kept at it—until his father made him quit—because he was a fighter and he loved trains with a fiery passion. There was only one thing Debs loved better than trains and that was the cause of the laboring man.

It was this cause that led Debs to jail. It also led him to join the Socialist Party and run for president on the Socialist ticket four times in a row, between 1900 and 1912, though he knew he couldn't win. His compassion for the laboring man attracted him to the social theories of

TEDDIFEROUS
INSANO
FURIOSO
EXPRESIDENSIS
HABITAT
OYSTER BAY

SEEING THE SIGHTS

*A political cartoon of 1915 portraying "Teddiferous"
Roosevelt as a caged animal harmlessly venting his
fury at President Wilson.* (Credit: New York Public
Library)

Karl Marx. From many podiums he taught that the world was divided into two classes of people, the working class and the capitalist class, that these two classes were locked in a death struggle, and that in the end the working class would win and capitalism would perish. He told workers they must join together to destroy the capitalist system because that system did evil things to their lives and to humanity in general. In a speech in Chicago in 1905, he explained what happens to a worker in time of depression:

Nobody wants your labor power, because it cannot be utilized at a profit to the capitalist who owns the tools, and when he cannot use your labor power at a satisfactory profit to himself he doesn't buy it. And if he doesn't buy your labor power you are idle, and when you are idle you don't draw any wages, and you can't buy groceries and pay rent; you can't buy clothing and shoes, and you begin to look seedy and shabby. By degrees you become a vagrant and a wanderer and lose what little self-respect you had. And then you hear that your wife has been evicted, and that is a thing that happens every day of the week. Your child is now upon the street and your former cottage home is deserted and you start out on what proves to be a never-ending journey. The road you are now traveling stretches wearily on, and from the hedges bark the dogs of civilization. You are a tramp.

Are there not thousands and thousands of tramps all over this country today? There were none a half a century ago. There is a great army of them now. They have been recruited in capitalist society; they are the products of the capitalist system.

On top of everything else, Debs said, capitalists caused wars. He believed that the heads of giant corporations in Europe and the United States controlled the government, the press and even the church, and that whenever war became profitable to them, they could have it at the snap of their fingers. The European war, he believed, grew out of the greedy competition between German and English businessmen for markets and investment opportunities in Africa, the Middle East and China. "Imperialism" was the popular word for this colossal struggle for territorial and financial control in undeveloped countries. The conflicting interests of rival bankers, supported by their respective governments, had made international news for 20 years or more. In Debs's view, once this mad scramble for profits had resulted in war, American businessmen had soon found ways to make money from Europe's necessity. England and France bought great shiploads of war supplies from American arms manufacturers, and when they ran out of money, America's giant banking firm, the House of Morgan, loaned them millions of dollars. It was common knowledge that on its last voyage the *Lusitania* had carried more than passengers: a cargo of 4,200 crates of American-made ammunition had been stored below deck.

The greed of American bankers and arms manufacturers was unbounded, said Debs. They wanted to sell quantities of guns not only to European governments but to their own government as well. Starting in 1915, they had financed a colossal publicity drive designed to frighten Americans into thinking that their country was doomed—the certain victim of Germany's ambitions for world conquest—unless the American army and navy were doubled in size and fighting power.

And now picture to yourselves, Debs told American workingmen, the horrors of the war that the capitalists had created.

The terrible war now raging in Europe has transformed nation after nation boasting of their civilization and Christianity into hideous slaughter-houses, where millions of our brothers have turned brutes and been shot like dogs; where king and kaiser and czar rule and bureaucracy and aristocracy and plutocracy, all rotten to the core and buttressed by dead men's bones, are supreme . . .

It wasn't necessary to be a Socialist to feel as Debs did about the war. The misery and pity of it was plain from the day it began. Two years later, ten million men had been killed, and the end was nowhere in sight. The plain facts of the situation argued more eloquently than Debs himself against involving America in Europe's bloodbath.

Since September 1914 when the armies in the west had dug themselves into opposing networks of deep, rat-infested trenches, the war had settled into a monotonous round of desperate raids and assaults on the enemy trenches, ending always in death, mutilation and failure. An attack, whether from the British and French side or from the German side, invariably followed the same pattern. Early in the morning, just before dawn, the attacker's heavy guns would open up all at once like the finale of a hundred Fourths of July. At first the guns aimed high at the enemy's own artillery and then lower down at the first row of trenches.

Toward the end of the barrage, the attacking soldiers, clutching grenades and bayoneted rifles, would leave the protection of their trenches, going "over the top" to begin the hellish run through the barbed wire entanglements across "no man's land" toward the enemy. The running distance between trenches averaged only 500 yards, but if you made it half way before being cut down by machine gun pellets and artillery shells, you did better than most. If the surviving remnant of the assault waves succeeded in seizing a trench, the enemy would counterattack from their second line of trenches and drive the invaders out. Typically, at the end of such a battle, the situation remained almost exactly the same. The only difference was the number of bodies, dead and dying, piled high amidst the mud and barbed wire of no man's land.

Witnesses to the slaughter expressed its folly and horror in different ways. A poet summed it up like this:

> Five hundred miles of Germans
>   Five hundred miles of French,
> And English, Scotch and Irish men
>   All fighting for a trench;
> And when the trench is taken
>   And many thousands slain,
> The losers, with more slaughter,
>   Retake the trench again.

A famous American newspaperman, Richard Harding Davis, wrote home about one early battle:

After the Germans were repulsed at Meaux and at Sézanne the dead of both armies were so many that they lay intermingled in layers three and four deep. They were buried in long pits and piled on top of each other like cigars in a box. Lines of fresh earth so long that you mistook them for trenches intended to conceal regiments, were in reality graves. Some bodies lay for days uncovered until they had lost all human semblance. They were so many you ceased to regard them even as corpses. They had become just part of the waste, a part of the shattered walls, uprooted trees, and fields ploughed by shells. What once had been your fellow men were only bundles of clothes, swollen and shapeless, like scarecrows stuffed with rags, polluting the air.

Though the generals in command soon saw clearly enough the futility of trying to crack open the enemy lines by frontal assault, they continued to send thousands of men to their deaths, in the hope that more of the enemy would die in the slaughter than their own men. Bleed the enemy white. That was the idea behind Verdun, the single most wasteful campaign of the war. The fortified town near the center of the French lines became the target for most of Germany's heavy guns and half of her army through most of 1916. A French officer on duty at the front gave an account of what he had seen:

Verdun has become a battle of madmen in the midst of a volcano. Whole regiments melt in a few minutes and others take their places only to perish in the same way. Between Saturday morning and noon Tuesday we estimate that the Germans used up 100,000 men on the west Meuse front alone . . . A full brigade was mowed down in a quarter hour's holocaust by our machine guns . . .
Even the wounded refuse to abandon the struggle. As though possessed by devils, they fight on until they fall senseless from loss of blood. A surgeon in a front-line post told me that, in a redoubt at the south part of the fort, of 200 French dead, fully half had more than two wounds. Those he was able to treat seemed utterly insane. They kept shouting war cries and their eyes blazed, and, strangest of all, they appeared indifferent to pain. At one moment

German cavalry overlooking trenches on the Western Front. (Credit: National Archives)

anesthetics ran out owing to the impossibility of bringing
forward fresh supplies through the bombardment. Arms,
even legs were amputated without a groan, and even
afterward the same men seemed not to have felt the shock.
They asked for a cigarette or inquired how the battle was
going.

The German generals abandoned the siege of Verdun
after having lost 400,000 of their own men in exchange for
500,000 French casualties. Verdun itself remained in
French hands. Almost a million lives had been wasted in
a fruitless struggle that brought no strategic change.

Among the few men who joined Eugene Debs in publicly
denouncing such horrors, and the war in general, was a
Nebraska politician, William Jennings Bryan. At a political convention in 1896, Bryan had spoken with such crackling power that the Democrats thought they could elect
him president. "Bryan, Bryan, the Mountain Lion," they
chanted, because when Bill Bryan spoke out against the
injustices done the common man by the big bankers and
railroad tycoons, his voice carried a country mile. Bryan
lost the election, but the Democrats had such faith in him
that they nominated him again in 1900 and again in 1908.
He was never elected president.

But he kept his faith in the common people, in the future
of America and in his hope for world peace—three ideas
that went together in Bryan's mind like the three sides of
a triangle. There had been a time before the sinking of the
Lusitania when, as Wilson's secretary of state, he believed
in the president as much as in the common people. But
Wilson's diplomatic notes to Germany, too weak to suit
Teddy Roosevelt, were too strong to suit Bryan, and he had
resigned from Wilson's cabinet to launch a one-man crusade for peace. Why had God planted America 3,000 miles
away from Europe, Bryan asked his audiences, if not as a
supreme example of peace for all the world to look at and
take hope from? At a peace rally in New York his voice
soared like a church organ when he said:

Some nation must lift the world out of the black night of
war into the light of that day when peace can be made

enduring by being built on love and brotherhood, and ours
is the nation to perform the task . . .

If civilization is to advance, the day must come when a
nation will feel no more obligated to accept a challenge to
war than an American citizen now feels obligated to accept
a challenge to fight a duel, and if that time must come
sometime, why not now? If some nation must lead the way,
why not our nation?

But how was anyone to know whether such vocal Americans as Bryan and Debs on one side of the war question,
or Marie Van Vorst, Archie Taber and Theodore Roosevelt
on the other, had won the battle for American public
opinion? On election day, November 5, 1916, after more
than a year of debate and argument and confusion following the *Lusitania* crisis, the American people were at last
about to come forward and be counted. But then, they were
voting not on the war question but on the re-election of
Woodrow Wilson. So how was anyone to know where the
people stood?

You could perhaps find out by listening to the songs they
sang. There was "I Didn't Raise My Boy to Be a Soldier,"
an antiwar song that became an instant hit the minute it
came out in 1915.

I Didn't Raise My Boy to Be a Soldier

> *I didn't raise my boy to be a soldier,*
> *I brought him up to be my pride and joy.*
> *Who dares to place a musket on his shoul-*
>   *der*
> *To shoot some other mother's darling boy?*
> *Let nations arbitrate their future troubles,*
> *It's time to lay the sword and gun away.*
> *There'd be no war today*
> *If mothers all would say,*
> *"I didn't raise my boy to be a soldier."*

But people were also singing "It's a Long Way to Tipper-
ary," the tune English soldiers whistled as they marched

off to war. And who knew whether people whistled and sang the songs because they loved or hated war, or simply because they liked the tunes?

And the newspapers? When a German submarine sank another ship, the *Sussex*, in March 1916 killing 80 of its passengers and injuring several Americans, Wilson dispatched another of his famous diplomatic messages. This time, however, he vowed that unless Germany gave absolute guarantees in its return note, the United States would take drastic action. For a moment, it looked like war. "Stand behind the President," cried the newspapers in unison, as if war was about to be declared. But then, for the second time, Germany pledged that there would be no more accidents, and the crisis passed. Most journalists accepted Germany's assurances as easily as Wilson. So there was little commitment in the newspapers either to peace or to war. And anyway, hadn't Debs and Bryan said that the newspapers spoke more for the big businessmen who controlled them than for the people who read them?

Perhaps, then, you could hear the voice of the people through their politicians. If so, in the ampitheater in St. Louis where the Democrats convened in August 1916 to nominate Wilson for re-election, it seemed that the people stood overwhelmingly for peace. The mere mention of Bryan's name brought the delegates to their feet. Tears streamed down Bryan's face as he listened to their cheers. The delegates were wild for peace. A newspaperman, Ray Stannard Baker, described what happened at the convention when the keynote speaker started reciting a list of former presidents who had refused to be provoked into war. The list began with President U. S. Grant:

"But we didn't go to war. Grant settled our troubles by negotiation just as the President of the United States is trying to do today."

The convention burst into wild applause.

The orator cited cases of violations under Harrison and Lincoln:

"But we didn't go to war."

He paused for the roar of approval . . .

He cited precedents under Pierce, Van Buren, Jefferson, Adams, Washington:
  "But we didn't to to war."
  The crowd was delirious with joy . . .
  "Go to it, Glynn. Give them some more!"

Unquestionably, here was a genuine demonstration for peace—but, looking closer, one found no sign of real commitment in it. The keynote speaker praised Wilson only for his *past* success in keeping the United States out of the war. There was no promise about the future, no assurance that the Democratic candidate would never take the country to war. Only the Socialists went that far, and they spoke for only one-fiftieth of the American voters, at best. And at their convention the Republicans demonstrated neither for peace nor for war—only for their nominee, Charles Evans Hughes.

The choice on election day, November 5, 1916, was between Hughes the Republican and Wilson the Democrat. The Democrats, Bill Bryan among them, tried to create the impression that a vote for Wilson was a vote for peace. "He Kept Us Out of War," ran the party slogan. An advertisement in the newspapers presented the choice this way:

You Are Working—Not Fighting!
Alive and Happy—Not Cannon Fodder!
Wilson and Peace With Honor?
or
Hughes with Roosevelt and War?

But the German-Americans, who wanted peace more than any national group, supported Hughes because Wilson's strong dealings with Germany over the *Lusitania* and the *Sussex* had offended them. Then, too, *The Nation*, a popular liberal magazine published by a leading pacifist, Oswald Garrison Villard, favored Hughes because Wilson had conceded to the bankers' demands for a big army and navy. It seemed to the voters that the candidates themselves had neither Gene Debs's commitment to peace nor the Colonel's commitment to war. Seventeen months after the *Lusitania* crisis, the situation was still "dulling and strange." And so on election day, 1916, the American people cast ballots for either Hughes or Wilson, but few were expressing an opinion about the war question, because both they and the candidates lacked the convictions of three men, a woman and a student.

6

A MESSAGE OF DEATH

"**S**top the presses!" shouted an editor of the *New York World* early on the morning after election day. A question mark had to be inserted in the banner headline. HUGHES ELECTED IN CLOSE CONTEST? read the corrected headline. The *World* had mistakenly assumed that when Hughes had won New York and the eastern seaboard he had carried the nation. But now the late returns from the West had come in, and they were solid for Wilson. In a few hours, Hughes's lead, once seemingly unshakable, had crumbled to nothing. Now nobody knew who would be president. It was the closest election of the century, and Americans would have to wait through two suspenseful days before its outcome was clear.

By underwater cable from New York to London, election reports sped across the ocean. An editor in the offices of the *Times* of London scanned the reports, then punched out on the typewriter a typically tactful editorial on "America and the Allies."

The American people as a whole have given the Allies an assistance which is recognized with gratitude by us and angrily resented by the enemy. They have lavishly supplied us with arms, with munitions, with equipment, with stores, with provisions for our armies, with raw material for our manufactures, with food for our people . . . Whatever may

be the course of America's domestic politics, and whoever
may be her President, we trust and believe that she will
continue to give the Allies the legitimate support, moral
and material, which she has afforded them throughout the
war.

The words about American support were true. Over-
night, at the beginning of the war in 1914, the United
States had become the arsenal of the British war effort.
Between 1914 and 1916, American trade with the French
and British had zoomed from $825 million to $3¼ billion,
while trade with Germany, $170 million in 1914, had
collapsed and shrunk to virtually nothing.

But the typical Londoner wanted a great deal more than
this. Since the *Lusitania* had gone down, he had hoped to
see American soldiers fighting in the trenches alongside
the British and the French. What had gone wrong, he
wondered. What had kept America out? Many decided it
was Wilson's famous patience and secretly yearned for his
defeat in the election. But by this time, even the English
could see that who became president mattered less than
what the German U-boats did to Americans at sea. Twice
now, Germany had given her solemn word that she would
not sink merchant ships without warning. If ever that
word were broken, even a man as cool-headed as Wilson
might feel honor-bound to go to war. So in England the
results of the election were watched with interest but with
a growing feeling that no matter who won, the United
States couldn't stay out of the war much longer.

The Germans were also keeping a close watch on the
American election. Almost to a man, they were bitter about
Wilson because he had allowed American food, guns and
ammunition to be shipped to England while the British
blockade was stopping everything, even food, from reaching Germany. Mrs. William Bullitt, wife of an official at
the American embassy in Berlin, entered in her diary an
account of the suffering of the German people as they
approached their third autumn of war:

The rains continue. In some sections of the country the
peasants are paddling around their potato fields in boats,

trying to save a portion of their crops. Our maid said yesterday, in tones of utter despair, that if the war went on much longer, there would be no men left, and if the rain continued, there would be no food left . . .

As the German people grew hungrier for both food and victory, the popular clamor to starve England into submission became ever louder and more insistent. James Gerard, the American ambassador to Germany, wrote in his diary in September 1916:

As these people get desperate the submarine question gets deeper and deeper under their skin. I really think that it is only a question of time . . .

As the Consul General at Hamburg has reported, serious riots have occurred there, two by the poor classes, mostly women, and one by students. The crowd shouted "Down with the Kaiser," called an end of the war, calling for unlimited submarine warfare against England.

The hate of Americans grows daily, if indeed it is possible to be greater.

Seeing all this, and reading angry editorials in the German newspapers, Germany's Chancellor Bethmann-Hollweg feared that it was only a question of time. For more than a year, he had done all he could to impress upon the kaiser the need for appeasing American opinion. But now, in the fall of 1916, his influence was slipping. The angry voices of the German people and the nation's military leaders, Gernerals Lundendorff and Hindenburg, were being heard above his own. If he wanted to keep his job, Bethmann-Hollweg realized, he would have to change his tune. Thus, in a letter of September 23, 1916, he told the kaiser:

Your Majesty's Navy promises itself a rapid success with the now largely increased number of U-boats . . . a success which would compel our principal foe, England, to make peace in a few months after the inauguration of an unrestricted submarine campaign.

Bethmann-Hollweg well knew that the "unrestricted submarine campaign" he spoke about almost inevitably meant war with the United States. But perhaps there was yet hope in the American election. Perhaps if Hughes won, he could find a way to free America from Wilson's rigid hostility to Germany's submarine blockade. Perhaps—but Bethmann-Hollweg didn't think so.

Neither did Woodrow Wilson. On election night, hearing the early reports that Hughes had won, Wilson said privately to a gloomy family circle: "There now seems little hope that we shall not be drawn into the War, though I have done everything I can to keep us out; but my defeat will be taken by Germany as a repudiation of my policy. Many of our own people will so construe it, and will try to force war upon the next Administration."

But suppose the early election news was wrong. If Wilson was reelected, could he do any better than Hughes to keep the United States neutral and at peace? "He kept us out of war," the Democrats had boasted during the presidential campaign. And it was true up to a point. But it could just as easily be said—and many did say—that Wilson's policies, far from keeping the United States out of war, were in fact pushing it in.

Wilson's critics accused him of only pretending to be neutral. In fact, they said, he had favored Britain in the war from the outset. They pointed out that the British were the first to declare a naval blockade and to search American merchant ships in ways that violated international law. Wilson had protested, but not vigorously enough to stop Britain's illegal blockade, and soon Germany's trade with America, so vital to Germany's war-making ability, was cut off almost completely. In 1915, Germany retaliated with a blockade of her own, using submarines to enforce it. Submarines were no more illegal than the mine-planting and naval searches of the British. And yet, over the sinking of the *Lusitania* and the *Sussex* Wilson came so close to threatening war that Germany abandoned the only tactics by which her counter-blockade could have worked.

Because the United States respected Britain's blockade while breaking Germany's, almost all of America's wartime trade began to find its way into British ports. Her trade in war supplies for the allied armies mounted into the millions of dollars and soon became the mainstay of the American economy. At the time of the election, England and the United States were practically business partners in war. It was an easy next step to become military partners as well. To Wilson's critics, reviewing the record, it looked as if the president had consciously tried to maneuver the country into war.

But those who knew Wilson personally knew that these charges were unfair. The thought of sending thousands of boys into battle filled the president with loathing. As he wrote in a letter to an English friend soon after the beginning of the war:

How terrible the whole thing is! It is like a nightmare. It depresses my spirits more than I can say, and our thoughts go constantly to you and your dear ones. May God keep you and bring us all into better days.

In addition, if the nation were to go to war, many of the domestic gains made in the previous years, upon which Wilson's political reputation rested, would be in jeopardy. An example was the hotly debated question of child labor. For many years, children as young as five years old had been working twelve hours a day in the dingy textile mills of Georgia, the suffocating coal mines of Pennsylvania, the reeking dye factories of Connecticut. Before she went to France, Marie Van Vorst had taken an interest in the fate of such children and had made many visits to the factories where they were employed. This is part of her conversation with a 10-year-old boy who lost part of his thumb working in a textile mill in Georgia:

"How old are you?"
"Ten."
"Are there any boys as young as you are in the mill?"
"Heaps of 'em younger," he affirmed; and then, lest I get an exaggerated impression, he corrected:
"There's none younger'n eight years old."
"Do you like to work?" I went on.

*His face was pitifully bloated and there was a lassitude
about his whole tiny person . . .*

"I sure do like work a heap better 'n doin' nothin'!"

"Wouldn't you like to go to school?"

*He looked at me as Cinderella might have stared,
sceptically, at the fairy godmother.*

*"I've never have been to school," he said, "but I reckon I'd
love that better'n anything."*

Unless war came, there was a growing chance that the
boy who lost his thumb in the mill and the more than a
million other child laborers in the United States might yet
escape the youth-destroying drudgery of the factory.
American public opinion wanted child labor stopped. By
1916, sensitive Americans had read enough stories in the
newspapers and magazines about children maimed and
killed in industrial accidents. They had begun to demand
laws, state and national, to prohibit the employment of
children under 14 and to compel their attendance at
school. Politicians in state after state had surrendered to
this overwhelming popular pressure for the abolition of
child labor by law. Slowly, children who had swept factory
floors since the age of five started filtering into the schools
to learn to read. And in the fall of 1916, shortly before the
election, President Wilson scored a great triumph when,
after a tremendous show of executive power, he won Con-
gressional passage of a national child labor law. It was one
of his last reforms, and many considered it the finest of his
presidency. Thus, after years of neglect and deprivation,
there was at least some hope for America's factory children. Unless war came to destroy it.

A war would change everything. In their passion to fight
a foreign enemy, most Americans would forget about the
factory children. They wouldn't care very much if the
Supreme Court treated the child labor law as it had
treated other liberal reforms and struck it down as unconstitutional. The president himself would be unable to
enforce his own law, because in wartime, men would be
called from the factories to become soldiers, and women
and children would be sucked in to take their places. The
law of 1916 had been the result of a titanic struggle. If the

Supreme Court were to invalidate it, who could say when and if the bill would ever be revived?

The prospect of sacrificing the child labor law made it even more unpleasant for Wilson to face the possibility that, despite his personal desire to maintain the peace, he might soon be appealing to Congress for a declaration of war. The pressures were mounting. There were still the constant appeals for the United States to defend the beleaguered citizens of France and Belgium. Then there was the balance-of-power thinking that held that the security of the United States might actually be jeopardized if German submarines were to break the balance of power in Europe and give Germany unrivaled sway over the Atlantic. Economic and political pressures were daily involving the United States more deeply in England's cause. And, perhaps ever more important in the idealistic reasoning that underpinned the president's thinking, there was the question of whether the country's image, her "honor," would suffer if she failed to react to the damage and insult done to her citizens and property in Germany's violation of the principle of freedom of the seas.

Wilson's sense of public duty beckoned him to war; his sense of personal morality beckoned him to peace. Two masters wrestled for possession of his mind. It had been that way ever since the *Lusitania* went down in May 1915. The tension was so great that the president suffered attacks of acute indigestion and nausea with every new crisis in diplomacy. To relax his mind, Wilson played golf regularly on the advice of his physician. But more than exercise, he needed a woman's comforting, sustaining presence. The feeling of bitter loneliness that had followed the death of his wife added to his present anxiety. Close friends were therefore delighted when the president met a charming Southern woman, Edith Bolling Galt, and began to spend much of his little spare time with her. Although he had been warned by political advisers that remarriage so soon after the death of his first wife might ruin his chances for reelection, he was a lonely man, and if it came to a choice between the two, he would choose remarriage. He and Mrs. Galt were married on December 18, 1915. Now, in the second Mrs.

Wilson, he had someone to nurse him through these days of agonizing decision.

But Wilson's agony remained nevertheless. For a man with so grave a problem, real relief could be found in only two ways. He could turn over the problem to someone else—Hughes if he were elected. Or, if the election fell on his own shoulders, he could cast off the burden of decision once and for all by committing himself finally to one thing or the other. He would act for peace. But if that failed, Wilson, like Chancellor Bethmann-Hollweg of Germany, would resign himself finally to war.

On November 7, 1916, two days after the election, Wilson and his new wife were playing golf together near their summer house on the New Jersey shore. From across the fairway, his physician and friend, Dr. Cary Grayson, ran up to him and breathlessly relayed the news. California was safely in the Democratic column. Hughes was beaten. The presidency was Wilson's for another four years.

Wilson returned to the White House with another attack of his old sickness. The time for final decision was at hand. He must try to bring the war in Europe to an end. He would write a note to the warring nations of Europe calling upon them to state their terms of peace. The hour was late; he would have to act fast. But before setting to work on the note, he would call his friend and adviser, Colonel Edward M. House, to the White House for a conference.

It was hard to think of Colonel House, a frail, soft-spoken little man, as either the colonel or the Texan that he was. He himself treated his military title as a joke, and he held no official post at all. Yet, because Wilson frequently consulted him and trusted him as he trusted no one else, the little Texan was among the most powerful men in America. Thus, a few days after the election, when the telephone rang in his New York apartment, House half expected it to be Wilson. He left for the White House at six o'clock the next morning. There, in a private conference, Wilson told him of his desire to write a peace note to the belligerents.

To the president's dismay, House called his plan impractical. He said he believed the British were in no mood to talk peace and the proposed move would deeply offend them. House wrote in his diary:

We then argued over and over again the question of what was best to do, I holding that for the moment nothing was necessary and we should sit tight and await further developments, the President holding that the submarine situation would not permit of delay and it was worth while to try mediation before breaking off with Germany . . .

But Wilson decided to act anyway. Racked with indigestion, stung by House's opinion, yet spurred by the thought that this was his last chance to keep the nation out of war, he worked feverishly on his peace note. He dispatched it at last on the day of his first wedding anniversary, December 18, 1916. He felt strong enough now to celebrate the double occasion by taking his wife for a walk on the golf course in the middle of a snow flurry. The president strode briskly across the new snow, his cheeks burning with the cold, his spirits restored by the knowledge that he had just taken a step toward peace.

Through the rest of December and well into January of the new year, 1917, Wilson and the American people waited hopefully for the Allies and Germany to deliver their terms for peace. The British were the first to respond to Wilson's note. The *New York Times* headline of January 12 read:

TERRITORIES OVERRUN, EVEN IN THE PAST,
TO BE RESTORED; EXPULSION OF THE TURK
AND REORGANIZATION OF EUROPE; THESE
WITH INDEMNITIES, ARE THE ALLIES' TERMS
OF PEACE

But such terms were unacceptable to the Germans. As the next day's headline proclaimed:

KAISER CALLS FOR REDOUBLED EFFORTS
AGAINST FOE WHO WOULD CRUSH

GERMANY; PRESS DECLARES ENTENTE'S DEMANDS MAD

The apparent failure of his peace note might have discouraged a man less stubborn and committed than the president, but it only stiffened his determination to make the belligerents talk peace, not conquest. Under an old green lamp, a favorite from college days, Wilson bent over a typewriter and, his mind overflowing with ideas on world peace, typed out one hopeful sentence after another. The kind of peace that Americans and all peace-loving peoples desired, Wilson wrote, was a "peace without victory . . . a peace among equals." From henceforth, there must be no more massive armies, no more interference with freedom of the seas, no more domination of one nation by another. "I would fain believe," Wilson wrote, "that I am speaking for the silent mass of mankind everywhere who have as yet had no place or opportunity to speak their real hearts out concerning the death and ruin they see to have come already upon the persons and the homes they hold most dear."

It was an inspired speech, a great speech, perhaps the best Wilson had ever written. At least Colonel House thought so when Wilson showed it to him just before delivering it to the Senate. The Senators thought so too, after they heard it. So did most of the nation and much of the world. The speech gave people hope that something good might come out of the war after all, in the form of a just and lasting peace. At the end of January 1917, their hopes and the president's were high that such a peace would soon be arranged. The headline for January 31 read:

BERLIN REPLY TO WILSON SPEECH COMING; MAY BE WILLING TO STATE PEACE TERMS, IF THERE IS A PROSPECT OF NEGOTIATIONS

But Wilson's efforts were all in vain. Count von Bernstorff, the German ambassador, had known this for two weeks, and his superior, Chancellor Bethmann-Hollweg, and Germany's Generals Ludendorff and Hindenburg had known it long before. A full month earlier, in fact, Germany's wartime leaders had met around a conference table and exchanged these words, as recorded in the official transcript of the meeting:

IMPERIAL CHANCELLOR *(Bethmann)* . . . *The experiences of the U-boats in recent months, the increased number of boats, the bad economic situation of England certainly form a reinforcement for luck. Taking it all round, the prospects of the unrestricted submarine campaign are very favourable. Of course those favourable prospects are not capable of proof. We must be quite clear that, judging by the military situation, great military blows are scarcely likely to bring us final victory. The U-boat campaign is the "last card." A very serious decision! . . .*

THE FIELD-MARSHAL *(Hindenburg)* . . . *We need the most energetic and ruthless action possible. Therefore the U-boat war must begin not later than February 1, 1917. The war must be brought to a speedy end . . .*

THE CHANCELLOR . . . *On America's eventual entry into the war, her help will consist in the delivery of food to England, financial assistance, the supply of aeroplanes and a force of volunteers.*

THE FIELD-MARSHAL . . . *We are already prepared to deal with that. The chances of the submarine operations are more favourable than they are ever likely to be again. We can and must begin them.*

THE CHANCELLOR . . . *Yes, we must act if victory beckons.*

Thus the decision was made to return to the policy that had sunk the *Lusitania*. Now it was von Bernstorff's unhappy lot to announce the fateful change in policy to the American secretary of state, Robert Lansing. Without saying a word, he handed Lansing a written declaration of Germany's intentions to sink instantly and without warning everything that ventured into the war zone, including American ships. Lansing later recorded his impressions of his last meeting with von Bernstorff:

As I finished my deliberate perusal of the papers, I laid them on the desk and turned toward Count von Bernstorff. "I am sorry," he said, "to have to bring about this situation, but my government could do nothing else."

I replied, "That is of course the excuse given for this sudden action, but you must know that it cannot be accepted."

"Of course, of course," he said, "I understand that. I know it is very serious, very, and I deeply regret that it is necessary."

"I believe you do regret it," I answered, "for you know what the results will be . . . "

"Of course, of course; I quite understand," he said, rising and extending his hand, which I took with a feeling almost of compassion for the man, whose eyes were suffused and who was not at all the jaunty, carefree man-of-the-world he usually was. With a ghost of a smile he bowed as I said "Good afternoon" and, turning, left the room.

Lansing grabbed his hat and, dashing to the White House, found the president in a state of shock. When Colonel House arrived the next morning, Wilson had not yet recovered. House wrote in his diary:

The President was sad and depressed and I did not succeed at any time during the day in lifting him into a better frame of mind. He was deeply disappointed in the sudden and unwarranted action of the German Government . . . The President said he felt as if the world had suddenly reversed itself; that after going from east to west, it had begun to go from west to east, and that he could not get his balance.

Wilson asked House if he thought there was any way he could avoid breaking off diplomatic relations with Germany, a step preliminary to war. House said there was no way; the president was honor-bound to send von Bernstorff home.

We sat listlessly during the morning until Lansing arrived, which was not until half-past eleven o'clock. The President nervously arranged his books and walked up and down the floor. Mrs. Wilson spoke of golf and asked whether I thought it would look badly if the President went on the links. I thought the American people would feel that he should not do anything so trivial at such a time.

In great governmental crises of this sort, the public have no conception what is happening on the stage behind the curtain. If the actors and the scenery could be viewed, as a tragedy like this is being prepared, it would be a revelation.

For both Europeans and Americans, Germany's declaration of unrestricted submarine warfare was the most startling single development since the *Lusitania* sinking. On hearing of it, Theodore Roosevelt went to his writing desk and dashed off a letter to the secretary of war asking to be notified the moment war should be declared. The same news sent a British naval officer flying up the stairs of the American embassy. Bursting unannounced into the ambassador's suite, he exclaimed breathlessly: "Bernstorff has just been given his passports. I shall probably get drunk tonight!"

Still the president hesitated. He was prepared to lead the United States to war only if he became convinced that her safety, her honor and her ideals demanded it. The situation in Europe and the danger from Germany's submarine warfare were insufficient proof. There had to be more.

It came soon enough. On February 25, Wilson received an urgent message from the American ambassador to England, together with a document of the most extraordinary character. This document, the ambassador explained, was a telegram written by a high official in the German government, Alfred Zimmermann, to the German ambassador in Mexico. It had been intercepted and decoded by British naval intelligence. Now, with the hope of bringing the United States into the war, the British government was transmitting its shocking contents to Washington. The telegram began:

WE INTEND TO BEGIN UNRESTRICTED SUBMARINE WAR-FARE ON THE FIRST OF FEBRUARY. WE SHALL ENDEAVOR IN SPITE OF THIS TO KEEP THE UNITED STATES NEUTRAL. IN THE EVENT OF THIS NOT SUCCEEDING, WE MAKE MEXICO A PROPOSAL OF ALLIANCE ON THE FOLLOWING BASIS: MAKE WAR TOGETHER, MAKE PEACE TOGETHER, GENEROUS FINANCIAL SUPPORT, AND AN UNDERSTANDING ON OUR PART THAT MEXICO IS TO RECONQUER THE LOST

TERRITORY IN TEXAS, NEW MEXICO, AND ARIZONA. THE
SETTLEMENT IN DETAIL IS LEFT TO YOU.

Wilson read the Zimmermann telegram with horror. He
made no effort to conceal his anger over Germany's intentions, and immediately released the document to the
newspapers. Printed in papers all over the country, the
Zimmermann telegram served to further heat up the
nation's temper.

Shortly afterward, in mid-March, 1917, came more incredible news, this time from Russia. There had been a
popular uprising in Moscow and St. Petersburg. The czar
had abdicated. A new Russian government was being
formed along constitutional, democratic lines. President
Wilson and his advisors had no illusions about the meaning of the uprising. It meant that there was starvation in
the Russian fields and factories and revolt in the army.
There was a new danger, even a likelihood, that the
Russian people would eventually compel their government to withdraw from the war. This would further en-
danger the balance of power, as Germany would then be
free to turn all her strength against the west and might
ultimately force the United States to enter the conflict and
bolster the flagging Allies.

Wilson still wished to avoid involving the United States
in the European conflict and naturally hoped that Russia
would stay in the war. But in one sense, the news from
Russia helped the president to reconcile himself to the idea
of war. Until now, he had been bothered by an ideological
flaw in the European situation. He could see democratic
America fighting on the side of democratic France, England and Belgium against imperial Germany and imperial Austria-Hungary. But he could not see America joined
with czarist Russia, a nation governed by a worse autocrat
than the German kaiser. Now that the czar had been
overthrown by revolution, however, the alignment of
forces—democracy on the one side battling autocracy on
the other—was clear-cut. America could join in such a war
with a clear conscience.

At last Wilson's mind was made up. To him, entering the
war now seemed the only way to protect American honor and

security and advance her ideals. Even so, he hated to ask Congress for the necessary declaration. A week before his scheduled address, he looked to his mild-mannered Texan friend for encouragement. Colonel House noted in his diary:

I told him a crisis had come in his Administration different from anything he had yet encountered . . . I said it was not as difficult a situation as many he had already successfully met, but that it was one for which he was not well fitted. He admitted this and said he did not believe he was fitted for the Presidency under such conditions. I thought he was too refined, too civilized, too intellectual, too cultivated not to see the incongruity and absurdity of war. It needs a man of coarser fibre and one less a philosopher than the President, to conduct a brutal, vigorous, and successful war.

It was drizzling on the evening of April 2, 1917, but the Wilson family and Colonel House hardly seemed to notice as they rode together to the Capitol building. In the House chamber, Wilson began reading his speech, breaking the oppressive silence of the room; but still the senators and congressmen, ambassadors and Supreme Court justices fidgeted nervously as they waited for the call to war. Finally it came:

With a profound sense of the solemn and even tragical character of the step I am taking and of the grave responsibilities which it involves, but in unhesitating obedience to what I deem my constitutional duty, I advise that the Congress declare the recent course of the Imperial German Government to be in fact nothing less than war against the government and people of the United States . . .

Everywhere in the great hall, people's eyes filled with tears and they stood and applauded the president for long minutes. The conclusion of the speech was also strong and deeply moving:

It is a distressing and oppressive duty, Gentlemen of the Congress, which I have performed in thus addressing you.

"America's Call to Arms": the complete war message
of Woodrow Wilson and the profile of its author as
created in 1917 by graphic artist Konrad Kail.
(Credit: New York Public Library)

There are, it may be, many months of fiery trial and sacrifice ahead of us. It is a fearful thing to lead this great peaceful people into war, into the most terrible and disastrous of all wars, civilization itself seems to be hanging in the balance. But the right is more precious than peace, and we shall fight for the things which we have always carried nearest our hearts—for democracy, for the right of those who submit to authority to have a voice in their own governments, for the right by such a concert of free peoples as shall bring peace and safety to all nations, and make the world itself at last free. To such a task we can dedicate our lives and our fortunes, everything that we are and everything that we have, with the pride of those who know that the day has come when America is privileged to spend her blood and her might for the principles that gave her birth and happiness and the peace which she has treasured. God help her, she can do no other.

Now the applause was deafening, and there were few dry eyes in the room. On the streets of Washington, citizens stood in the drizzle and applauded the president as he passed them in his car on the way back to the White House. But Wilson only frowned and, turning to a political aide, said sadly: "My message today was a message of death for our young men. How strange it seems to applaud that." And in spite of himself, the president's own eyes filled with tears.

7

TRANSFORMATION COMPLETE

There is no undertaking in human affairs quite so ambitious as waging war. Victory becomes the only important consideration to those in power, and everything, including individual freedom, is inevitably subordinated to it. To wage war efficiently, a government must command the total resources of the nation. Factories that once turned out shoes must now turn out soldiers' boots. Schools that once taught the virtues of peace must now teach the glories of war. The average citizen who seldom does more about politics than vote on election day must suddenly make repeated sacrifices for a political cause, the winning of the war. This transformation from peace to war must be total, and it must come fast.

How would the Wilson government accomplish this transformation in the United States? That was the big question in the spring of 1917. Some of the president's advisers were frankly worried. Too many Americans seemed unenthusiastic about going to war. The leading opponents of war asserted too many times and with too much conviction that if the American people were given a chance to vote on the question of war, a huge majority would be against it. And even those who supported the war had to acknowledge that there were millions of Americans who did not.

A week after the war resolution was adopted, President Wilson, by executive order, created the Committee on Public Information, under the directorship of a progressive journalist from Denver named George Creel. The purpose of the Committee was to bring an end to the vacillation in public opinion by convincing Americans of the rightness of their country's involvement in the war. Through the efforts of thousands of writers, artists, speakers and public performers, the conflict would be pictured as a "war to make the world safe for democracy," in which America was rallying to the aid of righteous democracies besieged by a power-mad kaiser and his militaristic clique. The idealistic speeches of the nation's leaders would be used to convince the country that America's participation was an act of noble sacrifice, and the most reliable of the atrocity stories coming from Europe would be dramatized to confirm the image of a uniformly evil enemy. The resulting crusade to win the allegiance of the American public has been called "perhaps the most gigantic propaganda campaign in American history."

But what of those who had already made up their minds that going to war was wrong? Among these millions were thousands of pacifists and Socialists to whom participation in the struggle in Europe was so abhorrent that they might be expected to sabotage the American war effort, or at least refuse to cooperate with it.

Arrayed against the war were three of the most influential political personalities of the day. There was energetic, bushy-haired, fiery-tongued Bob La Follette, Republican Senator from Wisconsin, who fought American entry into the war tooth and nail and, when the question came to a vote in the Senate, stood up with five others and said "No!" in a loud, defiant voice. There was William Jennings Bryan, the Democrats' great orator and favorite presidential candidate, who less than a week before the declaration of war continued to say that the American people wanted peace—even though the newspapers called him a traitor for saying so, and a mob in Baltimore chanted, "We'll hang Bill Bryan to a sour apple tree." There was, finally, the tall, lean, wiry-limbed crusader for the laboring man, Eugene V. Debs, who could be expected to carry his abiding hatred for all "capitalist" wars to the limit.

Less famous men, too, openly declared that they thought war an evil business and could never bring themselves to accept it. On Sunday, April 1, the day before Wilson was expected to deliver his message to Congress, the Reverend John Haynes Holmes, the pacifist minister of a church in New York, stood in the pulpit and told a stunned congregation:

War is an open violation of Christianity. If war is right then Christianity is wrong, false, a lie. If Christianity is right then war is wrong, false, a lie.

The minister said he still believed in Christ, and therefore:

When or if the system of conscription is adopted, I shall have to decline to serve. If this means a fine, I will pay my fine. If this means persecution, I will carry my cross. No order of President, no law of nation or state, no loss of reputation, freedom or life, will persuade me or force me to this business of killing.

Oswald Garrison Villard, pacifist owner of *The Nation* magazine, also stood firm. Lamenting the government's decision for war, he wrote in a letter to the president's secretary: "Believe me, I am ready for any concentration camp, or prison, but I am *not* at war and no one can *put me into war*—not the President of the United States with all his power."

The strenuous antiwar sentiment of the Socialists and other groups on the radical fringes of American politics caused government officials nightmares. The day after war was declared, the Socialist Party convened in emergency session, and reaffirmed its belief that America was going to war for the capitalist class at the expense of the working class, that big businessmen would get rich while the workers fought and died. Therefore, said the Socialists, "we call upon the workers of all countries to refuse to support their governments in their wars." Holding to the same position were the IWW's, or "Wobblies," as the members of the Industrial Workers of the World were called. The IWW was an organization of workers bent on labor organization and radical social change. They were constantly on strike, and for good reason. The wages they received for breaking their backs in America's mines and forests and orchards were just enough to keep their families hungry and in rags. The Wobblies were at war with capitalist society. They had no interest in fighting a war on the capitalists' side. And they didn't care if they were called traitors and thrown in jail; they were used to it. A third group who spoke for the working class, and therefore vehemently denounced the war, were the anarchists. Anarchists felt no allegiance whatsoever to the American government. In fact, they were opposed to the very idea of government and a national state. They expected to suffer for their beliefs and go to jail. It was part of their life as anarchists. A case in point was the story of the most famous anarchist of all, a woman named Emma Goldman.

The daughter of Russian Jews, Emma Goldman immigrated to America expecting to find a paradise of freedom and opportunity. Instead, working in a corset factory in Rochester, New York for pennies a day, she found only exploitation and poverty. She became an anarchist and publicly advocated the overthrow of the American government. For this, she spent a year on Blackwell's Island, a federal prison near New York City. After that, she became the editor of the anarchists' magazine, *Mother Earth*, in which she reminded workers of their obligation to fight the capitalist system. She denounced the European war and America's involvement in it as a capitalist plot and asked workers to think what it meant before fighting in it. As she wrote in *Mother Earth:*

We are told that the "freedom of the seas" is at stake and that "American honor" demands that we protect that precious freedom. What a farce! How much freedom of the seas can the masses of toilers or the disinherited and the unemployed ever enjoy? Would it not be well to look into this magic thing, "the freedom of the seas," before we sing patriotic songs and shout hurrah?

The only ones that have benefited by the "freedom of the seas" are the exploiters, the dealers in munition and food supplies. The "freedom of the seas" has served these unscrupulous American robbers and monopolists as a pretext to pilfer the unfortunate people of both Europe and America. Out of international carnage they have made billions, out of the misery of the people and the agony of women and children, the American financiers and industrial magnates have coined huge fortunes.

If the anarchists, the Socialists and the Wobblies, the pacifist ministers, editors and politicians continued to hold firm through the spring of 1917 against participating in the war, the possibility of President Wilson's conducting the war as a united national campaign would be undermined. But would they hold firm?

To expect long-term resistance of the middle-class American of 1917 was like expecting a child to run away from home. For in 1917, most Americans felt a closer attachment to their country than to any other cause. And they were bound by an urgent sense of duty. The idealism that pervaded Wilson's speeches struck sympathetic chords even in the hearts of some who had been opposed to the war at first. They believed that if their government declared war, their one duty was to help the country win it. To act otherwise would be treasonable. This kind of thinking went so deep that it made some of the most firmly committed pacifists and Socialists change their minds, or at least temporarily abandon their crusade against war. Villard, Bryan, La Follete all succumbed to this deep-seated sense of duty and attachment to country. Bryan, for example, no sooner heard news of the declaration of war than he dispatched this telegram to Wilson:

Believing it to be the duty of the citizen to bear his part of the burdens of war and his share of its perils, I hereby tender my services to the Government. Please enroll me as a private whenever I am needed and assign me to any work I can do.

Explaining his startling turnabout to a Southern audience, Bryan said: "Gladly would I have given my life to save my country from war, but now that my country has gone to war, gladly will I give my life to aid it."

Another thing that prevented idealists from continuing their antiwar crusade were Wilson's idealistic speeches. In his war message to Congress he had said that in going to war, America had no selfish ambitions to serve and sought no territorial conquest but was motivated by the purest principles of humanitarian service. Germany, with her ruthless submarine policy, had demonstrated beyond question that she was waging a war "against all mankind" and therefore America must enter the war so as to make the world safe for democracy. In Wilson's own words:

We are glad now that we see the facts with no veil of false pretense about them, to fight thus for the ultimate peace of the world and for the liberation of its peoples, the German peoples included; for the rights of nations great and small and the privilege of men everywhere to choose their way of life and of obedience. The world must be made safe for democracy. Its peace must be planted upon the tested foundation of political liberty. We have no selfish ends to serve. We desire no conquest, no dominion. We seek no indemnities for ourselves, no material compensation for the sacrifices we shall freely make. We are but one of the champions of the right of mankind.

In these magnificent phrases, an idealist could find reason to hope that once the war was ended and Germany was beaten, the major problems of the world, including the problem of war and peace, could be settled in a single stroke.

The remaining pacifists and Socialists who rejected the notion that a patriot must support a war and who distrusted Wilson's words, usually kept quiet just the same because they feared the censure and abuse of the prowar group. Agitated by rumors of internal and external danger, the American people were fast becoming an intolerant mob in April 1917. "We'll hang Bill Bryan to a sour apple tree," they chanted in Baltimore, and in Washington they hanged Bob La Follette in effigy when he voted "no" on the war resolution. They formed vigilante groups and, with the help of soldiers, sailors and policemen, broke up Socialist and pacifist rallies. They mocked any pacifist who stood by his convictions and made him feel strange and contemptible, an unnatural kind of creature, a disgrace to the human race. They could make a pacifist doubt his own position, because in 1917, almost everyone assumed that the natural thing for a young man to do in wartime was to enlist.

Almost everyone, for example, praised the efforts of Theodore Roosevelt and his four sons to get into uniform and go immediately to France. The Colonel himself was bitterly disappointed when Wilson spurned his offer to take personal command of four divisions of cavalry. But he was at least successful in getting his sons accepted. "My Dear General Pershing," wrote the Colonel, addressing the man Wilson had appointed to lead American troops to France, "I write to you now to request that my two sons, Theodore Roosevelt, Jr., 27, and Archibald B. Roosevelt, aged 23, both of Harvard, be allowed to enlist as privates under you, to go over with the first troops." The favor was instantly granted, and so two Roosevelt boys were promised a berth aboard the first American warship to sail to Europe. Through some influential British friends, the Colonel also placed Kermit Roosevelt in the British Mesopotamian Army. His youngest son Quentin, 20 years old and engaged to be married, wanted desperately to leave the boring college routine at Harvard where he was a sophomore, to pilot an army plane. He had a bad back, but thanks to his father, he was accepted at an air training school in Mineola, Long Island not far from New York City.

Quentin Roosevelt's eagerness to quit school and fight in France was typical of his generation. In a matter of weeks, the prestigious eastern colleges of Harvard, Yale, Columbia and Princeton lost great numbers of their students to army recruitment offices. Among those who left Princeton to enlist was a handsome, curly-headed, heroic-looking youth named Arthur Richmond Taber. Archie had left college once before to spend part of a year in the American Field Ambulance in France. He had therefore already seen the full misery and pity of war.

Archie had returned from France thinking that he might never go back. But he was an adventurer who yearned to fly an army plane, so Archie Taber of Princeton enrolled in the air school at Mineola right alongside Quentin Roosevelt of Harvard.

You didn't have to be in college to feel the urge to enlist and fly an army plane. Eddie Rickenbacker of Columbus, Ohio never made it past the eighth grade, but the adventurer in him was as strong as in any of Teddy Roosevelt's sons. Eddie seemed to have been born without a sense of fear. As a kid growing up, he had invented ways of looking death in the face. Once he had ridden a bicycle down a steep barn roof with an old umbrella in one hand. The umbrella was supposed to act as a parachute, but it failed and he almost broke his skull. Another time, Eddie had amused himself by counting the number of stunts that had almost killed him. He came up with the number fourteen, and that was before he started racing cars. He had as much luck preserving his life in cars as on flying bicycles. After several seasons of daredevil triumphs on the track, he was labeled the "Dutch Demon" by amazed sportswriters.

Eddie Rickenbacker's daring and his luck suited him for war. He knew this better than anybody. Between February and April 1917 he took time from his racing to get up on a soapbox and urge his countrymen to fight Germany. When war was declared, he volunteered to form a flying squadron of professional racing drivers, with himself in the lead plane.

By enlisting, young men like Quentin Roosevelt, Archie Taber and Eddie Rickenbacker became heroes of the hour to the American people, whose daily conversation and deeds were now filled with protestations of commitment and loyalty. Their songs, too, were beginning to appeal to American boys to show courage and join the fight. Instead of "I Didn't Raise My Boy to Be a Soldier," they were now more inclined to sing songs like this version of "Oh Johnny."

Oh Johnny, Oh Johnny, Oh!

*Uncle Sam is calling now for every
mother's son*

To go and get behind a gun,
And keep Old Glory waving on the sea.
Now prepare to be right there to help the
     cause along.
To ev'ry chap you meet when you're on the
     street,
You can sing this little song.
Oh, Johnny! Oh, Johnny! why do you lag?
Oh, Johnny! Oh, Johnny! Run to your flag.
You're country's calling, can't you hear? . . .

America's transformation from peace to war was almost complete.

But not quite. Nothing was certain until after Registration Day, June 5, 1917, when 10 million American boys between the ages of 21 and 31 were required by a new and controversial Selective Service Act to register their names with the government at local draft offices. Conscription was the old term for it, and it meant forcing men into military service. Conscription ran against the American grain. It hadn't been tried since the Civil War, and then it had provoked bloody riots in the streets of New York and elsewhere. Senators and congressmen warned Wilson that there would be riots worse than those of the Civil War if he tried to press men into service.

But Wilson wanted his troops recruited and trained in an efficient manner; the volunteer system was outdated by the ruthlessness of modern warfare. The efficient way to raise an army, said Wilson, was to issue to all young and able-bodied men a number, throw the numbers into a fishbowl, draw the numbers out of the bowl and draft into uniform the men whose numbers came up first. Over the protests of a Missouri senator named James A. Reed, who called the new system un-American, and of fighting Bob La Follette who called it undemocratic, the Selective Service Act passed into law. Thus, on June 5, 10 million young Americans were expected to report to the polling places in their towns and give their names to the state officials in exchange for a green card with a number on it.

Everywhere there were reminders of the forthcoming event. Within a border of tiny American flags under the headline "A Call to Arms," newspapers carried the President's official proclamation:

The day here named is the time upon which all shall present themselves for assignment to their tasks. It is for that reason destined to be remembered as one of the most conspicuous moments in our history. It is nothing less than the day upon which the manhood of the country shall step forward in one solid rank in defense of the ideals to which this nation is consecrated. It is important to those ideals no less than to the pride of this generation in manifesting its devotion to them that there be no gaps in the ranks.

At seven in the morning on June 5, factory whistles blew and church bells rang in every hamlet and city in the country. State officials sat expectantly at long tables ready to hand out a green draft card to anyone who lined up to register his name, address and age. This was the test day, the moment of truth for the government's war policy. Riots and disorders or even a less than perfect turnout at the registration places could seriously embarrass Wilson. The transformation of public attitudes so essential for waging war efficiently would then be shown to be incomplete.

But by noon on June 5, apprehension among state officials turned to rejoicing. The young men of the country were indeed turning out. They showed up with girls on their arms and swapped jokes with their buddies as they inched down the long lines toward the registration tables.

There was little trouble anywhere, and it was easily put down wherever it occurred. The newspapers reported that in Racine, Wisconsin:

John Robush, employed at the J. I. Case Tin Company was forced to kiss the American flag by 300 of his fellow employees today after he is alleged to have declared that he would not register and would not fight for the United States.

The man was made to crawl on his knees to the flag which had been spread upon the floor and after kissing it compelled to salute.

In Omaha, Nebraska the lone individual who dared to defy the draft was chased by an angry mob of 3,000 down the main street of the town. In fact, the only people who refused to register and got away with it were certain tribes of Indians. In Flagstaff, Arizona:

Navajo Indians drove an Indian agent and other Federal officers off the Government Reservation 100 miles northwest of here today. The Federal officers feared the Indians would go on the warpath if further attempts were made to register them.

At the same time, the Ute Indians of Colorado "refused to register under the Selective Service Act and spent most of the day dancing war and 'bear' dances in native costumes."

In other parts of the country, scattered groups of conscientious objectors who refused to register for the draft were quietly put in jail. But in general, things had gone so well for the Wilson government that it could afford to overlook the resistance of the Utes and Navajos and independent opponents of the war—at least for a time.

And so, on the whole, the administration had good reason to be jubilant over the success of Registration Day. The following official statement was issued to the press:

Nearly 10,000,000 Americans of military age registered for service in the army against Germany. The registration was accomplished in a fashion measuring up to the highest standards of Americanism . . . The Government officials who had professed the highest confidence in the patriotism of the young men of the nation, were deeply gratified at the result. It transcended their highest expectations.

It was spectacular, and a little strange, too, this almost perfect response to the government's call to arms. Ten million Americans, a tenth of the nation, had come forward to fight in a war from which neither they nor the country could derive any conceivable material good. In the wars of the past, Americans had fought in hopes of winning for themselves either some cherished political freedom, as in the Revolutionary War, or the conquest of new territory, as in the Mexican War. But this war of 1917 was different from the others. The president had said that America was entering it not for her own sake—for what could America gain that she did not already have?—but for humanity at large. The United States, having won freedom for herself, was going to set other nations free. She would liberate the Germans themselves from the autocratic rule of Kaiser Wilhelm and the Austrians and Hungarians from the imperial rule of the old Emperor Franz Josef. America was joining hands with the two great democracies of Europe, England and France, to vanquish and cast down the last vestiges of that ancient and outmoded system of power by which emperors and kings treated the common people as mere pawns in their schemes of empire. Defeat in war would lead automatically to the overthrow of these ruthless and irresponsible kaisers and kings. And then, in a perfectly democratic world, the foundations could be laid for a lasting peace. "The world must be made safe for democracy," Wilson had declared. And now America, with 10 million men committed and ready, was going to do it.

8

PRISONERS OF WAR

Registration Day assured Wilson of the loyal support of 99 Americans out of 100. But there was still that hundredth American who held out stubbornly against the majority and might seek to thwart its will. Even before the United States had entered the war, several large munitions factories on the East Coast, chief suppliers of the gunpowder England was buying from the United States, had mysteriously caught fire and burned to the ground. The cause for at least some of these explosions was clearly German sabotage. As early as February 1917, before war was officially declared, extra security guards were placed in American factories, and nervous citizens scanned the harbors and naval bases for signs of German submarines. Now that war had been declared, some people, the president included, feared that Americans sympathetic with the German cause might work with German saboteurs in attempting to undermine the war effort.

Much more dangerous than German sabotage, in Wilson's mind, was the opposition of the antiwar forces in America. The president feared that speeches and articles discrediting the United States government would undermine the nation's fighting morale and engender defiance of her laws. He believed that such agitation would seriously undercut the American war effort. France, England, Germany and Russia had all enacted emergency laws for dealing with espionage and subversion. At Wilson's urging, the United States followed suit. On June 15, 1917, it passed a law that threatened a 20-year jail sentence to anyone who "shall willfully cause or attempt to cause insubordination, disloyalty, mutiny or refusal of duty in the military or naval forces of the United States."

The Espionage Act, as it was called, was ostensibly aimed at hired agents of the German government, at spies and saboteurs. But the people who were to suffer most under its restrictions were innocent of any connection with Germany. They were simply people whose moral judgment and political conviction compelled them to fight America's decision for war. Most Americans at the time wasted no sympathy on this band of war protesters. They agreed with Wilson that in wartime no man was entitled to say and do things that could help the enemy and that anyone who did was a traitor and deserved a long jail sentence. And yet later, after the war, the traitors of 1917 and 1918 came to be regarded by some as great champions of individual liberty.

The Espionage Act ushered in a period of harsh censorship that lasted well beyond the end of the war. Numbers of magazines and periodicals were suppressed by the Postmaster General, some for the crime of printing mildly-worded articles questioning not the war effort, but some minute detail of its conduct. Thousands of people were sent to jail for their antiwar speeches and writings, and thousands more were frightened into silence. A man named Walter Mathey went to jail simply for going to an antiwar meeting, listening to the speeches and contributing 25 cents. When the Reverend Clarence Waldron told his Vermont Bible class that "a Christian can take no part in the war," he was sentenced to 15 years in the Atlanta penitentiary. John White, an Ohio farmer who complained about bad conditions in the army, was sentenced to 21 months. In dozens of schools the teaching of the German language was stopped; German textbooks were thrown on bonfires. People of German birth were roughed up by mobs, bullied, beaten, shoved in flour barrels and water troughs and forced to kneel and kiss the flag. Joe Spring, an Oklahoma waiter, was shot and killed for having allegedly made pro-German remarks.

If the stories of these unfortunates were not generally publicized, there were others who achieved a certain notoriety for their antiwar stance. Famous among those who mocked the war declaration, fought the draft law and defied the Espionage Act were a female anarchist, Emma Goldman, an aging Socialist, Eugene V. Debs, and a one-eyed Wobbly organizer, Frank Little.

Physically, Emma Goldman, with her graying hair and thin-rimmed spectacles, looked more like a grandmother than a firebrand. In every other way, however, she was a thorough rebel, wild as the wind. She had a crackling sharp mind and a crackling sharp tongue, and she took joy in using both. She thought American democracy a sham and said so. She was absolutely fearless. If any American could muster the courage to call the president of the United States a liar in time of war, it was Emma Goldman.

In fact, she called Wilson a liar repeatedly. In the anarchists' magazine *Mother Earth*, she made a mockery of the notion that America could be fighting a war for democracy when the government resorted to the most undemocratic methods for fighting that war. Conscription, for example, seemed to Emma Goldman the ultimate denial of freedom to the individual, and she was determined to fight it to the end. Together with another well-known anarchist, Alexander Berkman, an old friend whom she called Sasha, she organized a "No Conscription League." The first mass meeting of the league was called on the very day, May 18, that Congress was expected to vote the draft into law. Ten thousand radicals crowded into a New York meeting hall that day to hear Emma Goldman read the governing principles of the antidraft league:

We oppose conscription because we are internationalists, anti-militarists, and opposed to all wars waged by capitalistic governments.

We will fight for what we choose to fight for; we will never fight simply because we are ordered to fight.

We believe that the militarization of America is an evil that far outweighs in its anti-social and anti-libertarian effects, any good that may come from American participation in the war.

We will resist conscription by every means in our power, and we will sustain those who, for similar reasons, refuse to be conscripted.

It was difficult saying these things above the hoots and jeers of the drunken soldiers and sailors in the audience who had come to make trouble. But Emma Goldman outwitted them. She herself later described what happened:

Above the din the voice of a recruit shouted "I want the floor!" The patience of the audience had been sorely tried all evening by the interrupters. Now men rose from every part of the house and called to the disturber to shut up or be kicked out. I knew what such a thing would lead to, with the police waiting for a chance to aid the patriotic ruffians. Moreover, I did not want to deny free speech even to the soldier. Raising my voice, I appealed to the assembly to permit the man to speak. "We who have come here to protest against coercion and to demand the right to think and act in accordance with our consciences," I urged, "should recognize the right of an opponent to speak and we should listen quietly and grant him the respect we demand for ourselves. The young man no doubt believes in the justice of his cause as we do in ours, and he has pledged his life for it. I suggest therefore that we all rise in appreciation of his evident sincerity and that we hear him out in silence." The audience rose to a man.

The soldier had probably never before faced such a large assembly. He looked frightened and he began in a quavering voice that barely carried to the platform, although he was sitting near it. He stammered something about "German money" and "traitors," got confused, and came to a sudden stop. Then, turning to his comrades, he cried: "Oh, hell! Let's get out of here!" Out the whole gang slunk, waving their little flags and followed by laughter and applause.

A third meeting of the No Conscription League ended in disaster. Many of the younger men who came were arrested by police officers who ringed the hall in search of draft evaders. The next day, June 15, a federal marshal and deputies broke into the offices of *Mother Earth* and

arrested Emma Goldman and her friend Sasha on charges
of conspiring against the draft. She insisted on seeing the
officers' search warrants, but they said her statements in
the June issue of *Mother Earth* were all the warrant they
needed. Emma Goldman's tongue began working like a
whiplash. As she headed for the bathroom, one of the
deputies grabbed hold of her arm. She pulled herself loose
and said, "If your chief didn't have the guts to come up here
without a body-guard of thugs, he should at least have
instructed you not to act like one. I'm not going to run
away. I only want to dress for the reception awaiting us,
and I don't propose to let you act as my maid." Emma
Goldman continued to put her enemies to shame in the
courtroom, where she and Sasha conducted their own
defense. They mocked the prosecution's case so skillfully
that they had their audience—all but the judge and ju-
rors—laughing with them. Summing up her case, however, this courageous rebel spoke solemnly:

*So in a measure, I say, gentlemen, that we are greater
patriots than those who shoot off firecrackers and say that
democracy should be given to the world. But for the present
we are very poor in democracy. Free speech is suppressed.
Free assemblies are broken up by uniformed gangsters, one
after another. Women and girls at meetings are insulted by
soldiers under this "democracy." And therefore we say that
we are woefully poor in democracy at home. How can we
be generous in giving democracy to the world? So we say,
gentlemen of the jury, our crime, if crime there be, is not
having in any way conspired to tell young men not to
register, or having committed overt acts. Our crime, if
crime there be, consists in pointing out the real cause of the
present war.*

The jury filed out and in half an hour returned with the
verdict: guilty. The judge pronounced sentence—two years
in a federal penitentiary and a $10,000 fine. But, wrote
Emma Goldman:

*I was not through. "One moment, please," I called out.
Judge Mayer turned to face me. "Are we to be spirited away*

at such neck-breaking speed? If so, we want to know it now. We want everybody here to know it."

"You have ninety days in which to file an appeal."

"Never mind the ninety days," I retorted. "How about the next hour or two? Can we have that to gather up a few necessary things?"

"The prisoners are in the custody of the United States Marshal," was the curt answer.

The Judge again turned to leave. Again I brought him to a stop. "One more word!" He stared at me, his heavyset face flushed. I stared back. I bowed and said: "I want to thank you for your leniency and kindness in refusing us a stay of two days, a stay you would have accorded the most heinous criminal. I thank you once more."

His Honour grew white, anger spreading over his face. Nervously he fumbled with the papers on his desk. He moved his lips as if to speak, then abruptly turned and left the bench.

Emma Goldman then marched to jail with her head up.

Frank Little, too, would certainly have gone to jail—if he had lived long enough. But Frank, a Wobbly, had a special talent and mission in life that made the big corporations hate him and want him eliminated by whatever means. Organizing strikes and inspiring workers to join—that was Frank Little's specialty, and he was great at it. Even though he was lame in one leg and blind in one eye, he would go anywhere, do anything to participate in a strike and see that the men involved won unconditionally. He had worked with lumberjacks in the timber belt of the Great Northwest, with farm hands in the Great Plains, with miners in the Rockies and with roughnecks in the Texas oil fields. He could use his fists and knew the feel of a gun in his hand. He had seen the inside of countless jails. That was what it meant to be an IWW organizer, a radical, a Wobbly like Frank Little.

In theory, at least, a Wobbly was also supposed to think of the war in Europe as a capitalist plot. Until 1917, this was the official position of the IWW. But when war came to America and thousands of laborers who carried IWW cards enlisted, the executive board of the IWW failed to take a strong stand. William Haywood—Big Bill, as the Wobblies called their chief—said the IWW had troubles enough. The crusade against the war could only wreak havoc on the organization. Frank Little disagreed. He denounced the war openly, advised laborers not to register for the draft and recommended sabotaging America's war effort. Lumberjacks could drive spikes into their logs and farm hands could ruin the tractors and harvesters they operated. "Better to go out in a blaze of glory," Frank argued, "than to give in."

Famous last words. Three days after they were uttered, the body of Frank Little was cut down from a tree outside Butte, Montana. The copper miners in Butte had called Little to help organize their strike against the Anaconda Copper Company. It was strongly suspected, though never proved, that the copper company was behind the killing. The police in Butte were peculiarly unwilling to investigate deeply into the case, except to establish that around midnight of August 1, 1917, six masked men had broken into the boardinghouse where the Wobbly organizer was staying, bound his arms back, dragged him on a dirt road behind an automobile, put a noose around his neck and pinned a note to the dangling, mangled body—"Others take notice. First and last warning . . . "—the kind of message lynching parties of vigilantes used to leave in the days of the Old West.

So died the only leader of the IWW to speak of sabotaging the American war effort. Unfortunately for the IWW, however, Frank Little was not forgotten. Federal officials used his name and antiwar utterances and threats of sabotage to arrest, try and convict 101 Wobblies, Big Bill Haywood included, for violation of the Espionage Act. At their trial, Haywood and the others protested that their strike activities were in no way part of a grand design to sabotage the war. Yes, they admitted their hatred of capitalist wars. Some even admitted that they bore no love for America. As one Wobbly testified:

You ask me why the IWW is not patriotic to the United States. If you were a bum without a blanket; if you had left your wife and kids when you went west for a job, and had

*never located them since; if your job had never kept you
long enough in a place to qualify you to vote; if you slept in
a lousy, sour bunkhouse, and ate food just as rotten as they
could give you and get by with it; if deputy sheriffs shot
your cooking cans full of holes and spilled your grub on the
ground; if your wages were lowered on you when the bosses
thought they had you down . . . if every person who represented law and order and the nation beat you up, rail-
roaded you to jail, and the good Christian people cheered
and told them to go to it, how in hell do you expect a man
to be patriotic? This war is a businessman's war and we
don't see why we should go out and get shot in order to save
the lovely state of affairs that we now enjoy.*

The Wobblies protested their innocence even though
most of them knew that their case was lost from the start.
The American courts had a perfect opportunity in the
Espionage Act to crush their declared enemy, the IWW.
Though their best evidence lay in the statements of a
murdered man, they would doubtless consider it sufficient
to convict a hundred Wobblies. The defendants were thus
prepared for the verdict—30 years in prison for Big Bill
Haywood, from 5 to 10 years for most of the others. One
Wobbly leader, a black man, took the news so calmly he
cracked a joke about it. "The judge speaks bad English,"
he said. "His sentences are too long."

The IWW never recovered from the jailing of its leaders,
and Frank Little's stand against the war was largely
responsible. But the Wobblies admired Frank just the
same. After all, he had died for his beliefs as surely as any
soldier.

Unlike Frank Little, Gene Debs took a long time to
recognize that more was demanded of a genuine war
protester than an occasional word of criticism about his
government's policy. Until the spring of 1918, one full year
into the war, a few mildly worded articles were all that
had been heard from the old crusader. Of course, Debs's
health was bad, and he had his wife to think about. Also,
he considered himself a loyal American as well as a devoted Socialist, and it was hard not to support his country
in whatever venture she might be involved. Finally, he

saw other Socialists not only fall away from their earlier opposition to the war but actually rally enthusiastically behind the government. Even so, Debs felt guilty. Others of his friends had not surrendered. Instead, they stood on sidewalks amidst hostile crowds, circulating antiwar pamphlets and delivering antiwar speeches. Many of them were mobbed and beaten. In Illinois, a Socialist was lynched. Hundreds went to jail. A lifelong friend, Kate Richards O'Hare, faced a two-year sentence for an antiwar speech she had made.

The war now struck at Debs's conscience from two sides. As a gentle man, he recoiled at the thought of mass murder. "When I think of a cold, glittering steel bayonet being plunged into the white, quivering flesh of a human being," he said, "I recoil with horror. I have often wondered if I could take the life of my fellow man, even to save my own." Second, as a free- and liberal-thinking man, he hated to see anyone imprisoned simply for making a speech. It hurt most, of course, when the men and women going to jail for this ordinarily innocent act were his personal friends.

Therefore when proceedings were begun against Kate Richards O'Hare, Debs began to feel that he, too, must sacrifice himself. In a letter to Kate he said: "I cannot yet believe that they will ever dare to send you to prison for exercising your constitutional rights of free speech, but if they do ... I shall feel guilty to be at large." Soon afterward, Kate O'Hare was convicted and sent to the Missouri Penitentiary, where she and Emma Goldman became fast friends. At the same time, Big Bill Haywood and the IWW were standing trial, obviously on false charges. This was too much for Gene Debs. His conscience demanded that he support his friends to the limit, and the only way to do that was to speak out as forcefully as they had done and join them in prison.

He chose a blazing hot day in June 1918 to step up on a platform in a park in Canton, Ohio and deliver the speech he expected would get him arrested. First he spoke of his three friends in the Canton jail who were there for being good Socialists and speaking out against the war. He confessed his envy of them. "I would a thousand times rather be a free soul in jail than to be a sycophant and coward in the streets," he said. "They may put those boys in jail—and some of the rest of us in jail—but they cannot put the Socialist movement in jail." One by one, Debs reviewed the crimes committed by the American government against freedom and humanity. He mentioned the war only once, but he mentioned it with arms outstretched, his tall body bent almost double over the railing of the speaker's platform, so loudly that nobody in the audience, including the police, could fail to hear: "The master class has always declared the wars," he shouted. "The subject class has always fought the battles. The master class has all to gain and nothing to lose, while the subject class has had nothing to gain and all to lose—especially their lives." But the subject class was bound to win in the end, and then "this great cause triumphant—the greatest in history—will proclaim the working class and the brotherhood of all mankind." Gene Debs, the sweat pouring down his face, stepped back from the railing; the speech was over. The crowd, ignoring the police in their midst, cheered and waved their hats in the hot summer air.

Two weeks later, Eugene Debs was arrested for the things he had said on the platform in Canton. The judge sentenced him to 10 years in prison. At last the old Socialist warrior had won his chance to be "a free soul in jail."

Now Debs explained to the judge why he had allowed himself to be brought to this point:

Your Honor, years ago I recognized my kinship with all living things, and I made up my mind that I was not one bit better than the meanest of the earth. I said then, I say now, that while there is a lower class, I am in it; while there is a criminal element, I am of it; while there is a soul in prison, I am not free.

Seldom had a man faced a 10-year sentence with such radiant good will as Debs showed on the last day of his trial, September 9, 1918. He had done what he had to do; he had lived up to his courageous past. After months of torment and self-doubt, he felt free at last.

Debs was fortunate. He was old and famous when he took his stand. Thousands of admirers, including the Reverend John Haynes Holmes and publisher Oswald Garrison Villard, sent flowers, candy and good wishes to his prison cell in Atlanta. But others suffered alone. Numbers of young conscientious objectors who had refused to register for the draft were sitting in jail by themselves. Two, Joseph Arver and Otto Wangerin, went to court to challenge the government's authority to draft them. But their plea that the Selective Service Law violated human rights under the Constitution was brushed aside by the Supreme Court of the United States as "too frivolous for further notice." This same court, a few months later, struck down as unconstitutional Wilson's hard-won Child Labor Act. As the president had foreseen, now that the draft was in effect and manpower was short, children were needed to fill up the gaps in the labor force.

A conscientious objector was likely to pay dearly for sticking to his convictions. Ernest Meyer, a young student at the University of Wisconsin when the United States declared war, was a perfect candidate for the draft. But he didn't believe in the war and therefore pledged not to fight in it. Meyer came by his beliefs naturally. He had grown up in Chicago where his father, a German immigrant, had operated a Socialist newspaper. From his father he had learned the theory that greed for profits was behind most wars. He concluded in college that the circumstances behind the European war and America's entry into it proved the correctness of his father's theories.

He soon became involved at the University of Wisconsin in student rallies protesting the war and the draft. And, as editor of the student newspaper, he had written articles condemning the university for having fired and publicly disgraced a professor who had cracked a joke about patriotism. But now everyone around him—friends and professors as well as government officials—was pressuring him to wear a uniform and fight in a war he didn't believe in. Ernest consented at least to register for the draft, but after that, if his number came up, he was resolved to defy the army officials in everything—including all commands to put on a uniform.

Ernest was drafted in April 1918. His father was no longer alive to support him in his act of conscience. The university had expelled him for his antiwar position. His friends had deserted him—all except a girl companion who urged him to marry her so he wouldn't be entirely alone. "Write, write often!" shouted his bride of a week, racing after the train of draftees as it pulled out of the station. Ernest's letters to her give an idea of a man's capacity to stand alone against a crowd and endure anything for an ideal. The first one described what happened to him the day after his arrival at Camp Taylor, Kentucky:

This morning, after mess, we were lined up in the company street and after roll call army uniforms were issued. "You will each of you try on a uniform and if it doesn't fit, swap it with your buddies till you get a good fit," the corporal commanded. The forty-six rookies in my barracks stripped and began pulling on breeches, shirts, puttees and shoes. My outfit, neatly folded, lay on my cot. I sat on the cot quietly, though I was conscious of the blood pumping in my veins.

The corporal came briskly toward me.

"Snap into it, buddy," he barked. "We ain't got all day to wait."

My throat felt constricted, dry. I rose, steeling myself with effort.

"I am not going to put on that uniform," I said.

The corporal looked at me without comprehension.

"You put on that uniform, see," he repeated mechanically, "and if it doesn't fit, why, you can swap around and—"

"I refuse to put on that uniform," I said, a little louder.

When the corporal finally understood, he shouted for the sergeant. Other recruits gathered around expectantly as the sergeant stood before the defiant young man and bellowed: "I order you, private, to put on that uniform!" Again Ernest refused. "We'll see, you son of a bitch!" snapped the sergeant. "Follow me."

Ernest followed the sergeant to a spot on the dusty, sun-baked road outside the barracks while the 200 rookies tagged eagerly behind. Some shouted, "Lynch the bastard!" . . . "Shoot him!" According to Ernest's letter, the sergeant instructed the corporal to:

"Tell these loyal boys and this fellow here what we did to the last yellowback in the training battalion—that fellow who thought he was Jesus Christ himself."

"Yes, sir," said the corporal. "We provided the men with paddles and clubs, and we ran that slacker around the barracks and every man took a swing at him til he dropped."

Again, the uproar [of the angry crowd], wilder, more shrill. Again the sergeant ordered silence.

"One more chance," he said, turning toward me. "One more chance. Now will you put on that uniform?"

"I will not."

The clamor broke once more. The rookies closed in a tighter knot, their reddened, angry faces dust-streaked where the sweat ran . . . "The paddles, sergeant, break out the paddles!" And then, although the sergeant has given no signal, the shouting subsides. An orderly pushes his way through the jammed street, and behind him a man in captain's uniform . . . So the game will go on.

The sergeant and the corporal snapped to attention. The rookies straightened up, fumbling awkward salutes.

"What is wrong here, sergeant?" snapped the captain. He was young, wiry, polished, with steady, clever eyes and an even voice.

"We've found a slacker, sir, who refuses to put on the uniform."

The captain stepped up to me. "Mennonite?"

"No, sir," I answered.

"I didn't think so. You have no whiskers. Quaker?"

"No, sir. I belong to no church."

"Ah," said the captain coldly. "A new breed."

He turned to the sergeant.

"Sergeant, have this fellow brought to headquarters immediately. And clear the street."

Ernest thus narrowly escaped a beating. As he soon learned, others were less fortunate. The army sent him to live in a tent colony on the outskirts of the camp, where conscientious objectors like himself were forced to live out the war in quarantine as if they had an infectious disease. Here he was greeted by a group of solemn-faced, bearded youths in black woolen suits. They were surprised that Ernest had suffered so little.

"You are lucky," said one boy. "See there," he added, lowering his head and exposing what appeared to be a big red contusion on his scalp.
"What is that?" I asked.
"They pulled out my hair, yanked it out while a couple of soldiers held me. I don't remember what happened then. I fainted."
"They took off all my clothes except my underwear," said another, "and first they hit me with belts till I bled and then tied me on a chair and put me under a cold shower bath."
"And the officers were aware of all this?" I asked.
"I don't know. I don't think so. It was mostly the privates and there were a couple of non-coms [non-commissioned officers] too, I think. But you know we'd die first before putting on a uniform and killing a man," he added quietly. "We are Mennonites."

As Mennonites, these quiet boys took the Bible as their sole guide in life. They could not understand where Ernest's pacifism came from if not from the Bible. The boy whose hair had been pulled out read the Bible to Ernest daily in an effort to convert him, but it was no use. Except for the thought of his wife, Ernest was totally alone, unacceptable to the soldiers and unable to accept the fellowship of the Mennonites—an outcast.

The Army sent Ernest and the Mennonites from camp to camp, impatient to get rid of them or bully them into submission but unable to do either. In his fifth month of confinement, Ernest thought he almost preferred the excitement of that first day in camp, when they had threatened to beat him, to the monotony and loneliness and seeming futility of life on the stray edge of nowhere. "I have felt craven" he wrote:

Not for something I have failed to do, but something I have failed to endure. Though the worst may happen to me—imprisonment or torture, such as has been the fate of many of my friends—I am aware that all this would be but a scratch, a trifling ache compared to the unspeakable torments suffered by the soldiers in the trenches. I shudder for them, hope for them . . .

I think of my old friends in the trenches, Irv Wood, Carl Berger and the rest. It would be good to be at their side, good to endure to the end with them, if real truth or justice were served by my going.

But then Ernest remembered what he was doing there in the tent colony, a prisoner of war in his own country. It wasn't just to preserve his integrity, though this was part of it, but also to act out a hope and a belief that future generations would see future wars as he saw this one. The tone of Ernest's letter changed from doubt to affirmation:

I wish that we war objectors were not the miserable handful that we are, but a clamoring host, so that word of our existence would travel on the wind to all corners, and men everywhere would spike their guns and refuse longer to serve the warrior-imperialists who have betrayed them. We are so few now. But late, in the next war—for more will come, be sure of it—our ranks may be formidable . . . our folded arms all-powerful.

For one fleeting moment, Ernest Meyer forgot about his loneliness and boredom as he contemplated a distant future when thousands of young idealists like himself would act as he believed real patriots should act and refuse to bear arms.

9

I SENT OVER
MY FOUR BOYS

Of course, the "clamoring host" of conscientious objectors Ernest Meyer dreamed about was for the moment an illusion. Now, in 1918, Americans clamored only for victory. Win the War. Can the Kaiser. Beat Back the Hun. These were the slogans of the day. Save Food. Do Your Bit. Buy Bonds. Give Until it Hurts. These were slogans to live by in wartime America, 1918.

Open a newspaper, go to the movies or simply walk down the street and you were certain to see or hear some reminder of your patriotic duty in wartime. The Committee on Public Information saw to that. From Wilson's propaganda agency in Washington there rained down upon the nation a torrent of posters, pamphlets, speeches, movie reels and newspaper articles. The Committee on Public Information had agents in every town. It had postal clerks to tack up its posters, Boy Scouts to distribute its pamphlets and Four-Minute Men to deliver its speeches.

To the Four-Minute Men belonged the most glamorous and challenging assignment of all. Limited to speak for only four minutes at a time, these local orators would step into the spotlight on the stage of a movie house and, before the movie came on, attempt to fire their neighbors' enthusiasm for government bonds, food conservation, coal conservation, war savings stamps—anything the government said it needed to help with the war. In October 1917, for example, Four-Minute Men urged housewives and children in the movie audiences to enroll in the Food Administration, another special government agency, by signing "Food Pledge Cards." Americans could win the war, explained the Four-Minute Men, only if they ate less meat, sugar, wheat and pork—commodities desperately needed overseas. A model four-minute speech on Food Pledge Week, printed in the bulletin of the Four-Minute Men, went like this:

Here's a pledge card. See it!

It simply promises that you will live according to your conscience, nothing more. You promise merely to help stop sinful waste. No fees, no dues. Just a patriot's willingness to show good faith . . .

Who here, man or woman, is for helping the Food Administration? Who'll help and talk to friends about saving the waste of food? Who?

Hands up!

That's it—Look around.—See all the hands up.

Now, then, who's for this pledge card—(here it is)—merely a promise to live according to your conscience? Mrs. Woodrow Wilson was the first to sign. Who here wants that card?

Hands up!—Hands up!—Hands up!

Good! Now get your pledge card at the door when you go out, sign it and mail it before you go to bed tonight.

In order to save food for the war effort, women who joined the Food Administration agreed to use less wheat flour in the bread they baked. They used the following recipe to make a staple wartime loaf called Liberty bread:

LIBERTY BREAD

1 cup liquid
1 teaspoon salt
1 cup rolled oats
¼ cake compressed yeast in ¼ cup lukewarm water
2½ cups white flour

> Scald the liquid, add salt, and pour over the rolled oats. Cool slowly, letting it stand ½ hour. Add yeast and sifted flour, knead, and let rise until double in bulk. Shape into loaves; let rise in pan till light. Bake in a moderate oven from 50 to 60 minutes.

Besides Liberty bread, one spoke these days of Liberty pups, not dachshunds (the previous name sounded too German); Liberty sausages, not frankfurters; Liberty cabbage, not sauerkraut; and, of course, one tried to avoid an infectious disease called Liberty measles.

But the favorite topic of the Four-Minute Men was Liberty Bonds. Next to letters from sons in uniform, Liberty Bonds were the most cherished documents in the American household. First of all, they gave evidence of a man's loyalty and devotion to his country. In addition to that, the pressure to buy them was enormous. Four times in the course of the war, the government asked the American people for a loan of billions of dollars. Four times, state and town committees sent neighbors knocking on doors to chat with citizens about the money needed to finance the war and the necessity of "doing one's bit" for the country. Anyone who bought a bond was given a Liberty Button, which he wore on his lapel, partly out of pride, partly out of fear of what the neighbors might think if he were buttonless. "Lets play the game of button, button; who hasn't the button," suggested one newspaper, and millions of Americans played along.

Sometimes the mere wearing of a Liberty Button wasn't enough to satisfy the local committees; they were also interested in how much of a commitment the bond represented. The chairman of one such committee in Iowa advised local bond salesmen of a useful tactic for reluctant buyers:

> . . . you may have before you a slacker engaged in mercantile business and enjoying real prosperity. He perhaps may be defiant and arbitrarily contend that the purchase of two hundred dollars of bonds is his full share when you feel he should have taken ten times that amount. Just show him the picture of a real patriot; a widow whose only son is in the army and who now washes for a living

One of hundreds of war posters created both to raise money and arouse hatred for the enemy. The hand-print drips blood to suggest the many atrocious deeds of the German "Hun." (Credit: Steven Jantzen)

in order that she may use the allotment she received to help pay for five hundred dollars of her Government's bonds. Then ask his permission to take his picture and the picture of his store and his automobiles and his home in order that you may present the contrast at the next patriotic meeting, by throwing the pictures of the two characters on the screen with appropriate inscriptions. It is surprising how quickly he will see the light.

But such high-handed tactics accounted for a mere fraction of the $18 billion worth of Liberty Bonds bought by the American people in the course of the war, $4 billion beyond the government's needs. The bulk of the bonds were bought as a way of standing behind the young soldiers, the "boys" as they were fondly called, who were going to France to fight for a democratic world. American troops were only arriving in France at a trickle in 1917, but their mere presence in the theater of war was enough to stir the consciences of those at home. As the bulletin of the Four-Minute Men put it:

We here in America are not sleeping in mud to-night; we are not lying in caves with the murderous thunder and lightning above; we are not munching a cracker and a piece of cold bacon, nor standing gun in hand looking over a parapet into darkness with death lurking in front, by the side, and above.

Unlike those others over there, we are not privileged to give our all for America. We are privileged only to do the best we can . . .

The boys in uniform were the pride of their fathers and the envy of their younger brothers. Only through the Boy Scouts could teenagers know at least a little of their older brothers' glory. First of all, the Scouts wore the same wide-brimmed, four-cornered hat that American soldiers wore. Even better, the United States Committee on Public Information had chosen the Boy Scouts to act as President Wilson's official messengers of war. Each Scout had a manual giving him his orders. Counteract German propaganda, it said, with American propaganda.

As a democracy, our country faces great danger—not so much from submarines, battleships and armies, because, thanks to our allies, our enemies have apparently little chance of reaching our shores.

Our danger is from within.

Our enemies have representatives everywhere; they tell lies; they misrepresent the truth; they deceive our own people; they are a real menace to our country . . .

Here is where our service begins.

We are to help spread the facts about America and America's part in the World War.

We are to fight lies with the truth.

We are to help create public opinion "just as effective in helping to bring victory as ships and guns," to stir patriotism, the great force behind the ships and guns. Isn't that a challenge for every loyal scout?

The truth about the war, the manual continued, was contained in a series of pamphlets bearing such titles as "How the War Came to America" and "Why We Hate Germany." The Scout's job was to persuade 15 influential adults in his town to act as distributing agents for these government pamphlets. The Committee on Public Information reminded the Scout that manners and grooming were an important part of statesmanship. Said the Scout's manual:

A SCOUT IS CLEAN

Again you are the messenger of the Government to the people. Look the part. See that your face and hands are clean, shoes polished, badge on your hat, uniform correct and spotless. What you have to say will count more if you make a good impression.

A SCOUT IS COURTEOUS

Again you are the President's messenger, with a big message to carry. Act the part. Remember that politeness pays every time.

Even schoolteachers became involved with the government pamphlets. In 1918, war propaganda and war work had become an integral part of education. Daily, pupils from first through twelfth grade were taught and tested on the kaiser's crimes, America's idealistic war aims and the urgency of "doing your bit" for the country. "Doing your bit," to an adult, meant buying a Liberty Bond. To a child, it meant growing tomatoes and cucumbers in the school playground and buying "thrift stamps" at a quarter apiece. The 5,000,000 children who took time after school and on Saturdays to turn school yards, public parks and private estates into vegetable gardens wore arm bands initialed U.S.S.G.A. to show passers-by that they belonged to the United States School Garden Army.

The vegetables they grew and sold not only increased the food available for shipment to France and England but also earned money for buying thrift stamps. Fill a thrift card with these stamps and you received a war savings stamp worth $5. Fill a war savings card and you earned yourself a $50 Liberty Bond. For homework, pupils composed essays on the need for thrift in wartime. A Raleigh, North Carolina newspaper printed this prize-winning essay by a twelve-year-old boy:

HOW CAN I SAVE THINGS AND
BUY THRIFT STAMPS

We are at war. We have two enemies. One of our enemies is the Hun. We must go to France to fight him. Our other enemy is extravagance. We can and must fight that enemy over here in order to win the war. In these days money is energy. We need every available ounce of energy, therefore extravagance must be stamped out.

Pershing [commander of American forces] is fighting Fritz [nickname for a German]: McAdoo [Secretary of the Treasury] is fighting extravagance. The young men of the country are Pershing's army. We must save every cent and buy Thrift Stamps—that is our battle. We will have to struggle against every kind of enemy from moving-picture shows to gum drops, but we will win. We will have to wear half-soled shoes and mended trousers and dresses, and let our hair grow six inches, but the Hun will lose.

Two generals in France: the commander of the French army, Henri Petain (left), and the commander of the American Expeditionary Force, or A.E.F., John "Blackjack" Pershing. (Credit: National Archives)

Children and adults together thought of themselves as members of a great civilian army with an assignment in the war almost as vital as that of Pershing's troops: keep France and England from starving. In starkest terms, this was America's chief task in her first year of war, and it might in fact be fair to say that without the strenuous labors of the home army, the war would have ended in 1917 in German victory. The new German policy of unrestricted submarine warfare was working exactly according to plan. In the spring of 1917, German U-boats were sinking twice as many ships as Britain could replace, and unless the United States somehow made up the difference in ships, food and munitions, British reserves could hold out only a few months more. The Allies would then be faced with a dismal choice between starvation and surrender. Alive to the danger, Americans moved fast. As more and more housewives cut down their use of wheat flour, great bales of surplus wheat piled up on American wharves for shipment to the Allies. As families ate vegetables grown in their own war gardens, farm produce was freed for use in ration kits at the front. Laborers flocking to the seaports to build steel and wooden ships helped to replace those destroyed by German U-boats. Thus the Allies were kept from starving. And the German submarine campaign failed in its object.

But going into 1918, a children's army of vegetable gardeners would no longer be enough. From behind the trenches in Belgium and northern France, the German artillery was pounding the Allied lines with a ferocity matched only by the seige of Verdun two years before. And the Allied lines were buckling under the attack. Bled white by three years of war, the Allies needed more than food. They needed men. To Pershing's army, therefore, would go the task of smashing through to victory.

Americans of course understood that this meant death for vast numbers of their sons. It was no wonder that they treated as heroes the boys who had been drafted and sent to the training camps. The whole town turned out to cheer the local boys on the day they left for camp. There were banquets in their honor, prayers for their safe return and parades down Main Street from the town hall to the railroad station. The draftees in the parades rode in the back seats of automobiles and grinned at tearful girls who waved handkerchiefs at them. At the training camps, the YMCA and Knights of Columbus built and staffed recreation barracks for the boys. Girlfriends back home knitted socks and sent candy. And if a girl didn't know a boy in uniform, she might compose a letter like this one written by a young woman in the South:

After finishing this letter, I am going down and buy a newspaper, and the name of the first soldier I see in print— well, that's you—I am going to address and post that letter to you. I have never met you. But you don't think I am doing anything wrong, do you? Of course I am not signing this with my real name. But if you want me to write to you often, just reply to the address given below. Do you want me to tell you how the country looks down here in Dixie? Or do you want me to write you love letters, very warm and thrilling? What harm would that be? You would never see me. My mother would say that this was indiscreet, but I love to be indiscreet. Don't you—oh, my soldier boy? . . .

Nothing was too good for the boys! Did they crave cigarettes? Then, "HURRAH! HURRAH! HURRAH! THE MONITOR AND STATESMAN SOLDIERS' TOBACCO FUND IS OFF AGAIN" proclaimed one New Hampshire newspaper as it kicked off a drive to buy cigarettes for the troops. Did soldiers also crave wine, women and song? The wine and the women were off limits, but so many songs were sung that evenings in the army camps sounded like rehearsals for a musical comedy. Every night before taps, the men would crowd around the pianos in the recreation tent and sing for all they were worth. They might start off with the swaggering, half-nonsensical "Mademoiselle from Armentieres."

> *Mademoiselle from Armentieres, parlez-*
> *vous,*
> *Mademoiselle from Armentieres, parlez-*
> *vous,*
> *Mademoiselle from Armentieres*

She hasn't been kissed for forty years,
Inky dinky parlez-vous.

Then the camp pianist might play a string of blood-and-guts fighting tunes like "No Man's Land," "Long Boy," the "Coast Artillery Song" and the national favorite, "Over There." The song fest might conclude with the boys making fun of a lovesick soldier in "K-K-K-Katy."

K-K-K-Katy, beautiful Katy,
You're the only g-g-g-girl that I adore;
When the m-m-m-moon shines,
Over the cow shed,
I'll be waiting at the k-k-k-kitchen door.

At home, parents sang the same songs as their soldier sons and showed their pride by draping parlor windows with red and white service flags and sewing blue stars on them, one for each of their boys in uniform. Factories, banks and churches with employees or members in the army hung out service flags with row upon row of blue stars. And in Manchester, New Hampshire one lunch wagon was draped with a huge service flag honoring 67 of its regular customers who had gone off to war.

When a boy in the family died in the war, a gold star was sewn over the blue. At first such stars were rare. The first wave of Americans to land in France in 1917 saw no real fighting until November, and even then only three men were killed. Sadly, however, in the beginning of 1918, gold stars became more common. After three to four strenuous months in the training camps, America's draft army, 687,000 strong, was ready to fight. In the new year, 1918, troop ships were carrying young Americans to France at the rate of 50,000 a month. The song "Over There" had promised:

The Yanks are coming, the Yanks are coming,
The Yanks are coming over there.

Now at last they were there. Not in little bunches as before, but in great waves, relieving whole regiments of worn-out French and British troops. They arrived at a critical moment. The Allied armies were on the point of collapse. Three times in the spring of 1918 the Germans smashed into the French and British positions; three times the defenders yielded up their trenches, broke and retreated to the rear. For the first time in three and a half years of war, the armies were on the move. And they were moving in the direction of Paris. The fall of Paris was closer now than during the first German drive of 1914, when Germany had had to fight France and Russia simultaneously. Now, in 1918, Russia was out of the war. The Russian liberals had overthrown the czar in March 1917 only to be overthrown themselves by a Communist revolution in November. As his first act of statesmanship, Lenin, the new Red leader, had sued for peace. So a united German army was sweeping down on Paris. French generals and soldiers, weary and demoralized, were talking defeat as if it were only weeks away. Such was the state of affairs when the Americans arrived on the scene.

Whatever a person thought of American involvement in the war, it was clear that the arrival of the doughboys decidedly changed the war's course. Near the French town of Chateau-Thierry, a short distance from Paris, a division of Yanks took a stand on the banks of the Marne River, ground that the French had abandoned as lost. The Germans, feeling the momentum of their forward march, expected little resistance. But a division of Americans stood in their way and dynamited the bridge that led across the Marne. In so doing, the Americans cut off their own route of escape as well, and risked total annihilation. Under the cover of night, however, they escaped—with heavy casualties and enduring fame.

Not far from Chateau-Thierry, another wing of the German army was marching westward, unopposed, through a dense and rocky forest called Belleau Wood. A brigade of American Marines was rushed into the area with orders to "hold the line at all hazards." It was a hopeless assignment that only the Marines, trained to attack and never give an inch, could take seriously. There was no time to dig so much as one deep defensive trench. Instead, the Marines plunged into the wood, lobbing grenades at the killing machine guns that fired at them from behind boulders and stout trees. At the end of seven days, nothing was left of Belleau Wood but the stumps of trees, splintered at the top. But the badly-battered Marines didn't care, because they had cleared the wood of Germans and, in the process, showed that the German drive on Paris could be stopped. A month later, in mid-July 1918 French, British and American armies together began doing what a brigade of Marines had shown could be done at Belleau Wood. They attacked. And they won. Now it was the Germans who were retreating. The tide of battle had turned irreversibly.

The Allied troops needed the Americans more than they cared to admit. They needed them to fill gaps in the line; but most of all, weakened and dispirited themselves, they needed them for their cocksure spirit and dash. At the outset of the war, the French had felt sure they would win. So had the British. But in 1918, that spirit had been literally beaten to the ground. It took the green Americans, plunging into battle as if they were driving downfield for a touchdown, to revive the flagging hopes of the Allies.

If he was green, and a little fearful because unused to combat, the straight-talking, ever-cheerful American soldier of 1918 sent home letters that flamed with enthusiasm. Here's how Archie Taber, writing to his father from an air base outside Paris, described his luck as a novice pilot:

Since writing to you yesterday, the most extraordinary piece of good luck has suddenly fallen from the skies. I am located just outside of Paris and have been appointed as a "ferry" pilot, which means that I shall fly all over France . . . I shall have to take planes up to the front to any point along the line where our squadrons are, or fly to England or to the south of France . . . Of course this will be great fun; but the reason that I am so enthusiastic over this job is that it gives unparalleled training in cross-country flying, the experience of flying all kinds of machines, and the valuable foundation for any kind of work, of time in the air . . . Also you can appreciate that in such a job as this, one will have to be able to fly everything from a monoplane to a triplane, from the smallest to the largest and from the fastest to the slowest!

Archie regretted only that he would have to wait indefinitely before being assigned to the very *best* pilot's job, chasing German planes over the front line trenches. The waiting list for this most dangerous and exciting work ran to several pages.

Despite the waiting list, one of Archie Taber's classmates from the air school in Mineola had managed to achieve his dream. On June 6, 1918, Quentin Roosevelt had sent his mother a cablegram announcing his new assignment to the front. Some time later he wrote a letter describing his exhilaration at making his first contact with the Germans:

I got my first real excitement on the front for I think I got a Boche [German]... I was out on high patrol with the rest of my squadron when we got broken up, due to a mistake in formation. I dropped into a turn... When I got straightened out I couldn't spot my crowd anywhere, so, as I had only been up an hour, I decided to fool around a little before going home, as I was just over the lines. I turned and circled five minutes or so, and then suddenly... I saw three planes in formation. At first I thought they were Boche, but as they paid no attention to me I finally decided to chase them, thinking they were part of my crowd, so I started after them full speed. I thought at the time it was a little strange, with the wind blowing the way it was, that they should be going almost straight into Germany, but I had plenty of gas so I kept on.

They had been going absolutely straight and I was nearly in formation when the leader did a turn, and I saw to my horror that they had white tails with black crosses on them. Still I was so near by them that I thought I might pull up a little and take a crack at them. I had altitude on them, and what was more they hadn't seen me, so I pulled up, put my sights on the end man, and let go. I saw my tracers going all around him, but for some reason he never even turned, until all of a sudden his tail came up and he went down in a vrille [spin]. I wanted to follow him but the

*other two had started around after me, so I had to cut and
run.*

It wasn't only the airmen who wanted to see action. For
flier and foot soldier alike, the one place the American
fighting man wanted to be was at the front. Paul Howe of
Freedom, Pennsylvania wrote to his father that he could
put up with the discomfort of the trenches for "the thrill
of doing something worthwhile, of doing a little in the only
thing in the world that counts at present." He described
aspects of the daily routine:

*At night we must all be on the alert. Our patrols go out,
and so do the German patrols. Night is the danger time
from silent raids and from artillery prepared raids. During
the day inspections are made and then we sleep (if there is
time). Lack of sleep, plus wind and rain, cold and snow,
water and mud (always ankle-deep), shell-fire and casualties make life interesting. No one minds these things except
casualties and then the only outward sign is a very quiet
cursing . . . It [is] hard to see wounded men and men
wounded, yet no word of complaint. I've seen men laugh
with their eyes and nostrils filling with blood. I've seen
these men later in the hospitals. I saw them today. One man
from my company has an eye and an arm missing. One
man—a young man—a hot-blooded American, was found
with his throat cut after the raid. There was no need of a
hospital in this case. What a dirty shame it is! There is a
remedy, tho. The remedy is, kill Germans!*

Another soldier's letter told what it felt like to go "over
the top."

*This was war; I was finally in it. I can not say that I was
not excited; but I don't think I was afraid; only sort of
apprehensive. Thank God! It was night, and I overlooked
a great many horrors . . .*
"Please step high and over here. Thanks."
"What's matter? Wounded?"
"No. My pal is dying."
A little farther on a fellow lying on his back and looking

*straight up—and many such. Something seemed to grip
me; I wanted to run, but those fellows ahead of me were
cool enough; they were not afraid. Then we reached the
"jumping-over" trench. Our battalion was scheduled to
start at 6:30 A.M.*

*We were to have a barrage. Now I knew all about a
barrage, but had never seen one in action. Everything was
quiet after 3 A.M.; not a shell was fired. Fritz was sending
up lots of star shells, but that's his way. Six-fifteen, 6:25,
6:30. My God! All hell turned loose; my heart lost several
beats and then caught up and overdid itself. Some one
shouted, "Let's at them!"*

*Oh, it was a dandy barrage, and we walked over behind
it without much opposition and took our objective. I threw
my grenades at a couple of Huns in a bay and when they
exploded (both Huns and grenades) I slid into a trench,
and, according to plan, rebuilt the firing step. I prepared
myself in case of counterattack. I did not get a chance to
use my lovely bayonet.*

Like the boy with the "lovely bayonet," most soldiers at
the front craved an opportunity to kill. Their letters often
revealed the terrible capacity of war to blind the eyes of a
soldier to the humanity of his enemy. Fear, hardship and
the presence of death seemed to polarize the men's emotions, until they knew only desperate loyalty and desperate hate. A crumpled letter picked up on a muddy
battlefield and mailed to its American addressee in July
1918 presented a striking illustration of these two ex-
tremes:

*As we walked along the roads yesterday we could look
on either side and see dead Huns—boys who had died with
their boots on in defense of their country. Strange as it may
seem, my heart is hardened to a point where such a sight,
while pitiful, is a pleasure. For surely that is one way of
defeating our enemy—put him in his grave. Some boys told
me last night that the fields further up the line (about two
miles) are covered with dead Huns. As I write this letter I
feel somewhat nauseated from the odor of decayed bodies
in the immediate vicinity.*

Last night I witnessed a truly pitiful sight—the burying of our boys. The sight of our comrades being laid away for their final rest, garbed in a U.S. uniform, makes one's blood run cold and increases a passionate desire to deal out misery to the enemy . . .

On the whole, Americans were effective in this wartime task of dealing out misery. Some were spectacular. Among the most famous of the super-heroes was a racing driver from Columbus, Ohio—Eddie Rickenbacker. The newspapers were full of Eddie's daredevil feats as an ace pilot. One story read:

RICKENBACKER DOWNS FOE
Former Automobile Racer, Now
Airman, Fights Three Germans
WITH THE AMERICAN ARMY IN FRANCE, MAY 17
(Associated Press)

Another German aviator was brought down this morning in the American sector northwest of Toul. Details of the action have not been received but it appears that Lieutenant Edward Rickenbacker of Columbus, Ohio, answering an alarm soon after daylight, encountered three enemy planes. He attacked them and shot down one of them three kilometers inside the enemy lines.

In luck, Eddie outdid the proverbial cat with nine lives. Two enemy planes could swoop down on his tail and let go full blast with their machine guns within 50 yards of his open cockpit and still Eddie could wheel about, shoot the Germans out of the sky, return to earth for a few days and then go up again to repeat. After six months of this performance, Eddie had shot down 26 German planes, setting the American record and winning for himself a chestful of the most coveted military ribbons and medals.

But it wasn't all glory. Daily the newspapers carried sensational accounts of American heroism, but daily, too, they carried lists of the fallen. The lists grew longer with time. In March, 10 names was a lot for one day. In June, the death rate for American soldiers had risen to between 25 and 30 a day. In October, the daily average was close to 200. By the fall of 1918, families who had lost only one son out of three consoled themselves with the thought of the woman who had lost all five of hers. A father with more than one son in France couldn't help wondering which of his boys would be spared and which would go on the list.

Theodore Roosevelt had four sons in France. He was immensely proud of all of them. His three oldest—Theodore Jr., Archibald and Kermit—were fighting in the front-line trenches. The youngest, Quentin, was still serving in a daring assignment as an ace fighter pilot at the front. In his letters to France, the Colonel never failed to speak of the pride he felt in the heroic conduct of his four boys. To Ted Jr., he wrote: "Until you are an old man you will never be able quite to understand the satisfaction I feel because each of my sons is doing and has done better than I was doing and had done at his age—and I had done well."

The Colonel also had bitter words to say about Wilson's refusal to let him go to France himself. In his letters he told the boys that the only thing he was doing these days was puttering about making patriotic speeches and writing patriotic newspaper editorials, and generally feeling miserable the whole time because he couldn't do the manly thing and fight. On this point, anyone mean enough to want to do it could hurt him badly. At a patriotic rally in New York, a voice from the crowd interrupted the Colonel in the middle of his speech to shout: "Teddy, why don't *you* go over there?" For a moment, Roosevelt stood numb and silent. At last he said huskily, "I did my level best," and the audience cheered, "We know you did, Teddy. Give it to him." Then, leaning forward and wearing his angriest scowl, the Colonel said: "I have sent over my four boys, for each of whose lives I care a thousand times more than I care for my own—if you can understand that, you creature!"

On the morning of July 21, 1918, the lead headline in the *New York Tribune* read simply: QUENTIN KILLED. The omission of Quentin's last name was no oversight. The whole nation knew and loved the Colonel's children as it loved their father. Even the Germans respected the name of the young pilot they had killed. They buried Quentin themselves with full military honors, and marked the grave with the wreckage of his plane and a simple wooden cross. Somehow the Colonel kept from weeping. Better than anyone, he understood why Quentin had died. To his third son, Archie, he wrote: "Well, it is very dreadful, but, after all, he died as the heroes of old died; as brave and fearless men must die when a great cause calls. If our country did not contain such men it would not be our country . . ."

A newspaper cartoon pictured the Colonel standing with a hat over his heart in salute to a service flag bearing three blue stars—and one gold.

10

A MAN'S CHANCE

Private Henry Johnson, a black soldier in the U.S. Army, was awarded the Croix de Guerre for warding off a German assault with his bolo knife. Times must have changed, Johnson thought, because before the war, back home in the United States, there were no opportunities for blacks to win high honors—or even to win a measure of respect from the white majority.

American democracy did not exist for many black persons in the years before the First World War. To most, it was a beautiful but distant dream; to some, already disillusioned, it was a scandal and a lie. Poverty and humiliation seemed the permanent lot of a majority of blacks. But the United States' entry into the war kindled the hope that perhaps they might be given a fair chance at last.

Picture what it must have been like to grow up under the prewar conditions described by black author Richard Wright.

If a white man stopped a black on a southern road and asked: "Say, there, boy! It's one o'clock, isn't it?" the black man would answer: "Yessuh."

If the white man asked: "Say, it's not one o'clock, is it, boy?" the black man would answer: "Nawsuh."

And if the white man asked: "It's ten miles to Memphis, isn't it, boy?" the black man would answer: "Yessuh."

And if the white man asked: "It isn't ten miles to Memphis, is it, boy?" the black man would answer: "Nawsuh."

Always we said what we thought the whites wanted us to say.

Blacks who found they could bear this humiliation no longer, and cursed their tormentors instead of bowing to them, were likely to be beaten up or perhaps dragged to a deserted stretch of road and lynched.

Lynchings were commonplace early in the century. White mobs, most often in the southern states, hanged, shot or burned alive between 50 and 100 blacks—both men and women—every year. A quarter of the male victims were accused of having raped white women, but many of the charges were never proved. If a white man was accused of raping a black woman, he was fined $20 at the most and let off. And no white man ever went to jail for lynching a "nigger."

There had been a time immediately following the Civil War when blacks had stood a chance against white hostility. Protected by power-minded politicians as well as high-minded humanitarians from the North, they voted freely and even elected blacks to state offices. But southern whites, humiliated by their treatment under northern armies of occupation, vented their fury on blacks, and soon protection for local southern blacks was withdrawn. In the 1890s, southern legislatures enacted tricky laws whose only purpose was to strip blacks of their right to vote; and railroads, hotels and every manner of southern institution hammered signs on their facilities—"White Only," "Colored Only." Meanwhile, the federal government, instead of defending its black citizens, turned its back. Occasionally a northern politician might appoint a black postmaster in a small town or customs collector in a major port, but such token positions were the blacks' only recognition. And even the meager honor they afforded was stripped of its dignity when, in 1913, under Woodrow Wilson himself, post offices and other federal agencies were ordered to segregate their washrooms. Never since the days of slavery had black Americans been politically so powerless and socially so oppressed as on the eve of the world war.

Economically, too, they suffered. Some still picked cotton the same way their slave ancestors had done and for the same meager living. Others ground out their lives in low-paying jobs in mines and factories. True, they now worked as free men, in a legal sense, but no one kept in debt up to his ears is free.

The blacks who worked the cotton fields in those years seemed forever beholden to the "Lords of the Land," as Richard Wright called the white men in the old plantation houses who loaned black farmers their food, clothing and tools, taking in return most, if not all, of their crop. Autumn was the time of reckoning.

Southern blacks often thought about walking off the fields, but between 1900 and 1910, before the war, most of them remained where they were because there seemed nowhere else to go. Factory jobs in the South were always the meanest and the lowest paid; up North, blacks heard, things were better if they could find jobs, but most of the unskilled factory work there had already been taken by European immigrants.

Then the war broke out in Europe. Suddenly immigrants stopped flocking to the United States as in the past. Northern industrialists needed workers to replace them. Companies began to send agents south to attract black labor with promises of high wages and political equality, Northern jobs and Northern justice! For the first time since they had been freed from slavery, southern blacks had something to hope for on this earth. Richard Wright expressed the exultation of workers and their families as they prepared for the great migration to Chicago, New York, Philadelphia.

Lord in Heaven! God Almighty! Great day in the Morning! It's here! Our time has come! We are leaving! We are angry no more; we are leaving! We are bitter no more; we are leaving! We are leaving our homes, pulling up stakes to move on. We look up at the high southern sky and remember all the sunshine and the rain and we feel a sense of loss, but we are leaving. We look out at the wide green fields which our eyes saw when we first came into the world, and we feel full of regret, but we are leaving. We

scan the kind black faces we have looked upon since we first
saw the light of day, and, though pain is in our hearts, we
are leaving. We take one last furtive look over our shoulders
to the Big House—high upon a hill beyond the railroad
tracks—where the Lord of the Land lives, and we feel glad,
for we are leaving . . .

They left in droves, almost half a million black people
heading north into what seemed to be the Promised Land
during the first three years of World War I.

The prospect for equality for blacks looked even brighter
in April 1917 when the United States entered the war.
Surely, thought the leaders of the black communities, if
the nation was fighting for democracy abroad, it would
fight for it at home as well. If young blacks would rally to
the flag and fight bravely overseas, the nation might
reward them by granting to black people the rights and
opportunities they had so long been denied.

This was the hope, and for many young blacks, army life
promised almost as much as going north—steady pay and
escape from discrimination and drudgery. Young southern
blacks, therefore, were noticeably more eager to enlist
than southern whites. In one small town in Georgia, for
example, 23 of the 25 unmarried blacks volunteered for
the army at Wilson's first call.

Involvement with the war effort gave many of the
country's black citizens a greater feeling of sharing in the
national experience. A columnist for the *Washington Bee*,
a newspaper by and for blacks, was heartened by the
prospect of the effect this war could have on the future of
his people. He wrote:

I am one of those who believe that the present war will
settle forever the colored question in the United States.
There will be no North, no South, no East nor West. The
black man will be recognized and be treated as a man and
a brother. He will make a record of which the world will be
proud.

War or no war, however, racial discrimination and violent abuse of blacks continued. In 1915, a black citizen of

Memphis, Tennessee, Ell Parsons, was accused of raping and murdering a white girl. The white citizens of Memphis seized Ell Parsons, drove him to a spot outside town and chained him to an iron rail. Children were excused from school to witness the lynching that followed. When the lynching was over, the body of Ell Parsons was doused with gasoline and burned.

On July 2, 1917, another brutal incident occurred that engulfed an entire black community, this time in a northern city, well inside the "Promised Land." East St. Louis, an industrial town in southern Illinois, had a large black population for the period—6,000 in this city of 59,000 people. Many of the blacks had come up from the South to fill jobs vacated by white factory workers out on strike. The strikers had lost their bargaining position because of the influx of black workers willing to accept lower wages. Resentment was smoldering when, on July 2, local newspapers reported the slaying of two white detectives in a black neighborhood. Instantly violence erupted; white gangs formed and roamed the streets, setting fire to blacks' shacks and shooting at random in the black community. The records of the East St. Louis police told the story of a black girl who narrowly escaped being murdered that terrible day. She had been at home with her father when the rioting began.

Daughter and father were in house dodging bullets which were coming thick. Building at corner of Eighth and Walnut was occupied by whites. Some of the mob yelled, "Save it. Whites live there." Some of the rioters went to Eighth and Broadway and set fire to colored grocery store and colored barber shop. Man in barber shop escaped but the man and wife in store were burned up. By that time Opera House was on fire and flats on side and back of it. East end of Library Flats caught and heat was so great that father and daughter tried to escape through alley and up street to Broadway, but encountered mob at Broadway . . . Ran across street to Westbrook's home with bullets flying all around them and rioters shouting, "Kill him, kill him." Here daughter lost track of father. She beat on back door of Westbrook's home but no response, ran across alley to Division Avenue, ran on white lady's porch, but the lady would not let her in. Men were shooting at her for all they were worth, but she succeeded in dodging bullets. Ran across field and got in house and crawled under bed. Mob following right behind her, but lost sight of which house she went in and set fire to each end of flat. Rather than be burned to death she ran out and mob began shooting at her again. Just at that time a man ran out of the house, and the mob let girl alone and started at him. She fell in weeds and lay very quiet. Could see them beating man.

At last both the girl and her father found refuge in the police station, but when the father tried to explain what had happened, he himself was charged with rioting and jailed.

It was estimated that about one hundred blacks died in the East St. Louis riots.

Despite this brutal episode, black Americans still expressed support for their country and the war. *The Crisis*, a magazine dedicated to the civil rights of its black readers, urged unflagging support for the war effort because:

FIRST, *This is Our Country. We have worked for it, we have suffered for it, we have fought for it; we have made its music, we have tinged its ideals, its poetry, its religion, its dreams . . . If this is OUR country, then this is OUR war. We must fight it with every ounce of blood and treasure.*

SECOND, *Our Country is not Perfect. Few countries are. We have our memories and our present grievances. This nation has sinned against the light, but it has not sinned as Germany has sinned. Its continued existence and development is the hope of mankind and of black mankind, and not its menace . . .*

If black soldiers did not have the same chance as white soldiers, it was still a better chance than they were usually given in civilian life. First of all, over the protests of fearful southerners, blacks were drafted as liberally as whites and given the usual military training and equipment. To be sure, most of the officers in the segregated army camps were white, and yet, very importantly, the U.S. army, for the first time in its history, began to train black officers to command black troops. There was also to be an all-black army division, which would later demonstrate extraordinary courage and patriotism at the front. For the times, this was a cause for hope.

Young blacks in uniform struggled hard to make the experiment work. Insulted and discriminated against wherever they went, they held their tempers rather than risk an incident that could wreck the experiment. Perhaps it was most difficult in the beginning, particularly in the southern army training camps, where white officers jeered as the recruits, fresh from the farmlands and back country areas, came wide-eyed into the barracks, their belongings bundled up in old kerchiefs. From then on, the new troops were frequent victims of pranks and razzing. Sometimes they were run through the army's cold showers, to the amusement of all the nearby enlisted men. But they were determined to make good fighters, and after two months of training, they could march and drill and stick sandbags with their bayonets as expertly as the best soldiers in the army. The Buffaloes, an all-black regiment except for the white colonel in charge, set a record for marksmanship at Camp Upton, New York. In a parade in New York City on Washington's Birthday, 1918, the Buffaloes marched rhythmically down Broadway, chests high and heads back. A poet described them:

> *Down the street, between the waiting crowds, they*
>   *come—*
> *The Buffaloes,*
> *The Black Regiment!*
> *The band ahead,*
> *Thumping, crashing,*
> *Booming, smashing,*
> *"Onward Christian soldiers" fills the air.*
> *Black are the lines—*
> *All splendid black,*
> *Beneath the sharp bayonets,*
> *Under the high waving flags;*
> *A long way they have marched,*
> *Down the long years they have come,*
> *Through suffering and despair,*

From Africa to Manhattan,
From slavery to freedom,
Men—citizens—at last!

Even the South was applauding its black troops as they marched off to the European war. An editorial in a South Carolina newspaper remarked: "The Negroes of South Carolina are standing by. They are loyal, they are earnest, they are zealous. Sometimes they shame us in their exhibition of their understanding of the causes of this war and their determination to support the Government throughout." An observer at a camp in West Virginia told a familiar tale of the Southerner who changed his opinion about his black brothers once he saw them in uniform.

There is a shout outside: "Hey! Look what's coming!" We step outside. Down the road, thump-thump, thump-thump! There is no sound in all that great cantonment save the beat of marching feet and the creaking of packs. The black men know they are on their way abroad. They are a solemn-looking lot. A minister steps out to the edge of the embankment overlooking the road down which the troops are marching, and calls out shakily: "Good-by, boys. God bless you! God take care of you, boys!" . . .

A big Mississippian, standing near, swore growlingly under his breath, gulped, and cried.

"I'm done talking against niggers," he declared huskily. "Those boys have been damn fine soldiers here, an' if they ever get back from France, I'm big enough to lick any man who don't give 'em a square deal."

Young black soldiers seemed to be boosting the reputation of their race even before sailing for France; once there, they were eager to set examples of bravery and service. Two black soldiers, Henry Johnson and Needham Roberts, were the first Americans to win the Croix de Guerre. Their outfit, the 369th Infantry, saw more continuous duty on the front lines than any other American regiment. During World War I, when all regiments clamored for service at the front, such duty was considered an honor. In April 1918, the 369th, sent into action ahead of most regiments, was the envy of the entire American army. Other black infantry regiments, on the other hand—the 367th (Buffaloes), 370th and 371st—waited a long time before they saw any fighting. From June to September they were stationed around Verdun in the extreme southeastern sector of the line, while white troops were winning all the glory at Belleau Wood and Château-Thierry. Occasionally they could hear the distant thunder of guns on their left— French guns softening up the German trenchworks for the combined French and American assaults.

Through the summer of 1918, while many American regiments waited to see real action, the Germans were losing the ground they had won in the spring at the terrible cost of 100,000 lives. The tables had now turned decisively. German strength was ebbing without any prospect of renewal at the same time that the Yanks were landing in France, a million of them by July, another million by November. Inside Germany, the people were losing heart. They were hungry after four years of British blockade; hundreds a day were dying of starvation. Many were shouting for the kaiser to end the war on whatever terms. The American regiments, pouring into battle, had infused the Allied forces with energy and hope. And the German army kept retreating, mile after bloody mile.

By the fall of 1918, the war was almost over. Every day, the British on the north, the Americans on the south and the French in the center reported another French town liberated, another German squadron captured, another battle won. Entering November, rumors of an armistice flew thick as bullets. It was almost too late for the famous black regiment, the Buffaloes, to see any service at the front. But at the last hour they were called. A black reporter was there to watch them:

I was at the front when the drive began—this last battle of the world war. I was thrilled, and inspired by the enthusiasm of our men, and their eagerness to get into battle. The thundering of the big guns, the terrific explosion of death-carrying shells—hell opening up—served only to inspire our colored soldiers with a grim determination to maintain the race's traditional fighting reputation. As I

A squad of black Americans in action, 1918. (Credit: National Archives)

retraced my steps over the battlefield, the awful field of carnage, and saw the havoc German shells had wrought; saw lifeless, blood-bespattered bodies . . . lying on the dark and bloody field; saw the maimed and mangled living, the natural feeling of sorrow, of anguish, of pain, was made endurable only by the thought that our men—our colored soldiers—were in it to the end, that they fought like heroes, died like heroes, died like martyrs.

And then the news flew down the trenches: an armistice had been signed. When the soldiers learned that it was all over, and when the guns up and down the line stopped firing for the first time in what seemed an eternity, nobody cheered. Slowly the soldiers rose up over the tops of their trenches and looked out toward the enemy. Not a bullet came from the other side, not a sound. A Frenchman finally broke the stillness. "La guerre est finie" (the war is over), he exclaimed, more in astonishment than in joy. Blacks and whites together passed the word: "The war is over! The war is over!" One black soldier, a Buffalo, was also heard to say something else, something perhaps only his companions in the regiment could understand. Summing up the war's special meaning for his people, he cried, "We came and won a man's chance!"

It would remain to be seen how much participation in the Great War had actually won for his people.

11

HALLELUJAH!

In the excitement over news of an armistice, a minister from Concord, New Hampshire told a reporter from the local newspaper: "This is the greatest day that the world has known since the birth of Christ." And on such a day, no one thought to contradict him. If ever there had been a time for overstatement, it was now. Church bells rang; factory whistles shrieked; people danced in the streets. America had done it. The war was won. The boys were coming home. Peace reigned throughout the world. It was the greatest day since the birth of Christ. Hallelujah!

Hot, excited words clattered off a typewriter in the *New York Tribune* offices as a reporter attempted to describe the hysteria that broke over the world's biggest city at lunchtime on Thursday, November 7, 1918.

A whistle high above the pinnacles of office buildings spoke loudly at one o'clock yesterday. New Yorkers turning from luncheon tables and dinner pails toward the rest of the day's work, paused to listen.

As they hesitated another siren and another took up the call. The noise swelled from individual tootings into a buzzing roar that swept northward over the city in a great ever-increasing wave of sound.

Then, to the crowds who stood wondering and trying to stifle the thought that was uppermost in each mind, came the answer to 5,000,000 unspoken questions. It came from the throats of thousands of newsboys, running, paper-laden, through the streets and shouting the most splendid tidings the city has ever heard.

"Germany surrenders!" they cried. "Peace! War is over! O-h-h-h extra!"

Then the city—the great proud city that had not wept aloud when she saw her sons march away, who had stifled her tears when she read the casualty lists—felt a great sob catch in her throat and throwing aside all reserve wept and laughed openly and unashamed.

In the streets men gripped the extras and then stood, moist eyes averted, swallowing hard . . .

The whole town by now was roaring and echoing to the blasts of the sirens. Craft in the river added their voices to the cry of victory. In the streets automobile horns bawled and wailed triumphantly . . .

Work was forgotten . . . The vast majority of the offices and industries gave their workers a holiday. In the others the employees stampeded down stairways, never waiting for elevators, and joined the massed ranks of men and women who surged up and down the avenues or collected in open spaces to shout and cheer and laugh and cry like so many madmen . . .

Over their heads hung the bluest of skies, in which great clouds of bits of paper fluttered like butterflies. Above them the flags whimpered and whispered. The people did not look where they were going. They did not care who spoke to them nor who reached out a hand to drag them into one of the lockstep processions that tramped up and down the street, clamoring like children at play.

For the first time in four years New York was utterly happy . . .

From New York's Harlem to San Francisco's China-town, it was the same story—swarming throngs of deliri-ous people dancing, kissing, weeping, laughing.

Oh, it was a glorious thing to be a schoolboy that day and tear up old test papers and scatter them about the classroom, and dump wastepaper baskets out the school windows, and race out onto the streets and stuff fistfuls of confetti down strangers' backs and snatch old women's hats and throw them in the air, and kiss a girl smack on the lips and beat on the lid of a garbage can, and all the time yell like crazy. That's what schoolboys did to celebrate, and adults did their best to imitate. The *New York Times* reported:

Men wore their overcoats wrong side out, they solemnly smashed derby hats and set the rims back on their heads; men put on women's hats and women men's hats; men and women walked about draped in American flags.

When the celebrants tired of yelling, they sang. "Hinky Dinky," the "Marseillaise," "America, America"—it didn't matter what. Around one lamppost could be heard a lusty fragment of "Over There," and as the crowd whirled around someone else could be heard singing the "Star Spangled Banner": ". . . And the rockets' red glare, the bombs bursting in air . . ." And just as one joined the singing ". . . gave proof through the night . . ." the crowd spun around again.

And so it went all afternoon and evening. Nothing could stop the cheering, not even news that the reports of an armistice were all wrong.

No armistice, in fact, had been signed at lunchtime, November 7, 1918. The German generals were only talking about surrender; they had not signed yet. So the war went on, but so too did the dancing and the singing. What did it matter if they were celebrating an illusion? It was too much fun to stop, and at least an armistice was in the making. "Well, they're going to sign it pretty soon," one man explained to a reporter, "and I'll just keep on celebrating until they do." The next day, kids tumbled merrily in the piles of ticker-tape and torn paper that littered the streets, and dockworkers took the day off to parade down New York's Broadway.

What did it mean, this total insanity over false reports? The editors of *The Nation* puzzled over possible answers:

What did it mean? Something like this might have been expected in Paris or Berlin or London where the war has

Celebrating the armistice in Paris. Notice the French flags carried by Americans and an American flag carried by a Frenchman. (Credit: National Archives)

*borne so heavily upon everyone. But why here? Was it
merely the elation of the crowd? Was it relief that the loved
ones abroad were safe? Or just the American joy at winning
a great game? Or, in addition to all this, is it possible that
the war was not so popular after all with the rank and file?
We confess to being completely baffled in our efforts to
analyze something which in fervor, excitement and sud-
denness could surely never be surpassed.*

The most intriguing possibility was that, aside from the
mothers and wives, who wanted the boys home more than
anything, people were celebrating the dawn of a new era
marked by world-wide democracy and eternal peace. After
all, this was supposed to be the "war to end wars." The
British had invented this slogan back in 1914, and as time
went on, more and more Americans had adopted it as their
own until, by 1918, eternal peace and the winning of the
war were assumed to go hand in glove.

Some even made the linking of the two ideas an article
of religion. The Baha'is, a religious sect founded by a
Persian mystic, believed that Isaiah of the Bible was
talking not about Jesus Christ but about President Wilson
when he prophesied: "For unto us a child is born, unto us
a son is given, and his name shall be called Wonderful
Counselor, Mighty God, Everlasting Father, Prince of
Peace . . .". Wilson would usher in the millennium by
winning the war for the Allies and then creating a form of
world government that would keep the peace for all time.

The war meant something almost as dramatic to many
who took themselves to be ordinary Christians. "This has
been Christ's war," commented the *Los Angeles Times*.
"Christ on one side, and all that stood opposed to Christ
on the other side."

In the public imagination, the forces of good had scored
a stunning and perhaps permanent victory over the forces
of evil. Not everyone agreed with the Baha'is that President Wilson represented the second coming of Christ. But
about the "devil's man" there was no disagreement. In the
United States, in the last days of the war, almost everyone
hated the kaiser. In his flowing silk cape, twirled ox-bow
mustache and ornate spiked helmet, he seemed the pic-

ture of villainy. His downfall, when it came, would signify the triumph of democracy over autocracy, of right over might, of good over evil. Dethrone the kaiser, maybe even hang him, and the evils of the world would die with him. Now that the devil himself was about to be exorcised, it was no wonder that people wept and threw their hats away over reports, even mistaken ones, that Germany had surrendered.

There was some question about whether people would have enough enthusiasm left over from the false armistice to celebrate the real one when it finally came. But early one morning, when the church bells pealed again and the factory whistles hooted, rousing them from their sleep, American citizens were as full of songs and kisses as ever. The day was Monday, November 11, 1918, and this time it was certain—the Germans had signed the papers. In the streets of Berlin, people were rioting against the German warlords. The kaiser had run away to Holland, a coward afraid to face punishment. Americans heard the news as they threw on their bathrobes and raced into the bracing autumn air, cheering their heads off and smacking frying pans with soup ladles. From then until midnight, it was the same wild party all over again, except that they had run out of paper and ticker-tape. So from the hotel windows, they threw down coins and dollar bills instead.

There were accidents, too. In Detroit, an airplane pilot buzzed the crowds, got his wing tangled in an American flag and went spinning to his death. In New York, drunken sailors wanting to make a big noise fired pistols in the air, killing one person and wounding five others. But the cheering crowds intended no harm to anyone but the kaiser. On the streets of every American town, the kaiser was tortured and killed symbolically in a hundred ways. His face was caricatured in chalk on the sidewalk and stepped on a million times. A stuffed dummy of him bearing a sign saying "Sock Him One!" was dragged through the streets of Philadelphia and, placed in the stream of traffic, finally pounded to shreds.

The reasons for this violent merriment were complex, but the *Keene Sentinel,* a New Hampshire newspaper, ventured to explain them:

And why are we glad? . . . It is because the Almighty God has triumphed over his enemies. Because right and freedom have beaten might and slavery. Because kindness and the brotherhood of man have won a great victory over cruelty and the power of the sword . . .

So we celebrate the return of peace. And well we may, for this is the beginning of the greatest era the whole world has every known. There must never be another war. There will not be. And with the reign of the Lord of Peace forever more what wondrous blessings shall come to the world—to you and to me.

12

MESSIAH AT PARIS

"**D**earest Little Ma," wrote Archie Taber, sitting on his army cot in France and wondering how to tell his mother that he'd really rather stay over there than return home. Finally he just blurted it out:

I'd like to do almost anything but come home. Please forgive me for writing so bluntly, for I don't mean it so; I should love to go home for a short time to see you, Papa and Kit, if I could return again soon afterward; but since that is impossible, I'm anxious to stay over here during this most stupendous epoch-making period of the world's history. I don't want to fall into what I shall consider in later years as a mistake; here I've the opportunity of seeing this whole show from the front-row, so to speak; I feel it would be foolish to lose the chance by going home too soon, especially when there are millions of persons in America who would give anything to be over here.

It was true. Everybody, it seemed, wanted to go to Paris just to be there when Wilson came over to remake the world. Doubtless that was Wilson's purpose—to substitute one world order for another, an order governed by ideals instead of money and international competition. After January 1918 when he delivered another of his world-shaking speeches, who had not heard of Wilson's incredible 14-point plan for peace? "Open covenants of peace, openly arrived at," said the first point. "Absolute freedom of navigation upon the seas," said the second. "The removal . . . of all economic barriers" between nations, said the third. There would be drastic reduction of armaments everywhere. Africans and Asians then subject to European colonial domination could look forward to eventual independence. Points six through thirteen sketched in the boundaries of a new Europe. Out of Austria-Hungary, now a sprawling and hopeless ruin, would come a cluster of bright new nations. The French would get Alsace-Lorraine; the Poles would have a new Poland; the Italians would have an expanded Italy; the Slavs would have a new country altogether. And then, to crown the whole and keep it forever intact, Wilson had concluded with his most beautiful dream, a "league of nations" in which member states pledged to settle their disputes peacefully. Leaflets bearing translations of Wilson's peace plan were scattered wholesale across Europe.

Great and awesome things, therefore, were expected of the American president when he came to Paris, and it was no wonder he was regarded as a kind of savior. An American newspaperman, Ray Stannard Baker, remembered how they worshipped Wilson in Italy long before the armistice:

> . . . I can say truthfully that the commanding interest in Italy at that time was centered upon what Woodrow Wilson was saying, and what the Americans proposed to do in the coming peace conference . . . In the cities many walls were placarded with the words of Woodrow Wilson, headed: "Parole Scultore di Wilson" [Famous Words of Wilson] setting forth extracts from his recent speeches. His portrait appeared in innumerable shop windows. I collected a large number of post cards with his picture and many with quotations from his addresses. An Italian editor I knew told me that he had actually seen candles burning underneath Wilson's picture in home windows. I should doubt whether there was ever before in any country such a demonstration of faith in the leader of another nation.

Paris in November and December 1918 was like the center of the world. Into its streets and hotels flocked delegations from the 27 nations that at one time or another had entered the war against Germany. From as far away as Brazil and Japan they came to draw up a treaty and settle the war in the greatest peace conference ever held.

Then dawned the morning of Wilson's entry into Paris. Cannons boomed the city's greeting as the American president and his wife emerged from the railroad station and rode in separate carriages past cheering throngs. The scene formed a vivid picture in Mrs. Wilson's memory. Years later, she wrote:

The Champs Elysees was cleared all the way to the Place de la Concorde, with solid lines of French soldiers standing like sentinels on either side. Captured German cannon, hideous in their spotted camouflage, sent a chill down my spine. But today there was no place for them in a gay world, for Paris was wild with celebration. Every inch was covered with cheering, shouting humanity.

For one giddy month, the Wilsons whirled through a never-ending round of banquets, speeches, changes of clothes and cheering crowds. And flowers, always flowers. On a trip through London, the flowers that rained down on them were thrown by British schoolgirls draped in American flags.

Evenings they passed in princely company. The king and queen of England invited them to dinner, and they sat over gold plates and ate with gold forks and gold knives and gold spoons. The king and queen of Italy showed them the sights of Rome.

Wilson, however, infinitely preferred the people's bouquets to the kings' dinners. The flowers that landed in his carriage were a sign of his power as well as a tribute to his person. Without them, his peace plan was lost. But with oceans of flowers symbolizing his immense popularity, he could sit down with the other statesmen at Paris and say he spoke for the peoples of the world and demand that they base the treaty with Germany upon his League of Nations and his Fourteen Points. He especially needed the backing of the people because at Paris he faced two of the craftiest bargainers in world politics, England's Prime Minister David Lloyd George and France's Premier Georges Clemenceau, neither of whom cared a pickle for his Fourteen Points. Germany must pay; that was their motto.

Lloyd George, stumping for reelection at the same time Wilson was touring Europe, promised to charge Germany a monstrous fee for war damages. Clemenceau was even more intent on reparations, hoping to seize Germany's rich coal fields for France. It was the same old story of winner-take-all, that to Wilson's mind only caused more wars. The only way to a lasting peace, he insisted, was to write a just and humane treaty, a treaty pleasing to all nations, Germany included. That was the principle behind the Fourteen Points.

Why punish the Germans, Wilson asked. The war had already killed 2,000,000 of their men and wounded another 4,000,000. They had suffered hunger and starvation. They were sick of war and to prove it had expelled the kaiser, replacing him with a fully democratic government.

William Allen White, an American newspaperman, traveled through the Rhineland, the western portion of Germany then occupied by American troops. Everywhere he observed an astonishing spirit of friendliness between American soldiers and German civilians.

The children seemed to take to these grinning cheerful-looking American boys as big brothers. They [the soldiers] had no trouble with the civilian population, for they were natural-born fraternizers and couldn't help it. Certainly they were guests and not conquerors. The hosts and the guests were as polite to each other as a basket of chips. The American soldiers tipped their hats to the old men and the women, and even the officers got off the walks for the women and the old men. They played with the young girls on the sly in spite of all the rules of the G.H.Q. [General Headquarters].

Did Clemenceau and Lloyd George propose to poison this friendly spirit by "squeezing Germany until the pips squeak," as one Englishman had put it? This was to be a "war to end wars." Had the British forgotten?

If they had, thought Wilson, it was his job to remind them. Rather, it was his solemn duty. He must have a just peace. Above all, he must have a League of Nations. It was the only thing that could justify the hideous sights he and Mrs. Wilson had seen in the Red Cross hospitals in Paris.

Recuperating in the hospitals were American soldiers who had gone blind or whose legs were now stumps or whose faces had been shot away. Wilson remembered the speech he had made at Christmas-time to about 2,000 American soldiers in a remote village in eastern France. He had promised them then that he would win the kind of peace their heroism deserved. The men had stood there ankle-deep in the mud, and few had applauded. How would it be possible for Wilson to leave the peace conference and return home empty-handed?

Nearly a month had gone by since Wilson's triumphal entry into Paris. It was now early in the new year, 1919, and the peace conference was about to open. Until now, though Wilson had skirmished with Lloyd George and Clemenceau once or twice, he had entrusted the weight of the diplomatic war to his respected adviser, Colonel House. House had done well. The day Wilson returned from Italy, he had won Clemenceau's consent to a League of Nations. According to House's diary, Clemenceau "placed both hands on my shoulders and said, 'You are right. I am for the League of Nations as you have it in mind and you may count upon me to work with you.'" So Clemenceau, whom the French called "Tiger" because of the ferocity of his politics, had softened on the League. An encouraging beginning, but now Wilson had to press his advantage and win swift adoption of the League while the peace delegates were still dazzled by his flower-strewn European tour.

He worked around the clock. His wife seldom saw him. Either Clemenceau and Lloyd George came to see him in his study, or he went out to meet them in Colonel House's hotel suite. Occasionally newspaperman Ray Stannard Baker, on his way to interview Wilson, would see the three great men strolling out of the president's study. This is Baker's description of Clemenceau:

I see him now—his body as solid, square, strong, as though built out of oak wood; his short legs, his great drum of a chest, his head set far back and held very erect, the bald top of it the color of old yellow parchment, and freckled. He always wore gray cloth gloves, in conference and out—I never saw his bare hands; got up at 4 o'clock in the morning and went to bed at 8 or 9 in the evening, and, though 78 years old, was able, within two weeks after being shot by a would-be assassin, to return to the conference.

Between conferences, Wilson was besieged by anxious callers from the little countries of eastern Europe, Asia and Africa whose national destinies were at the mercy of the big powers—England, France and America. Baker wrote:

I remember vividly one such delegation which symbolized the instinctive trust of the smaller nations in America, and their hope in Wilson's leadership. I came into the office one morning and found two as extraordinary figures as ever came to Paris. They were Polish peasants clad in their own home-spun natural wool, red-embroidered, with Cossack caps of shaggy black fur. They had with them a Polish priest, who spoke French, to tell what they wanted. It seems that they were from a little pocket settlement of Poles in the mountains of northern Austria, and that in the boundaries that had been set at Paris they were included in the new nation of the Czechoslovaks.

They told, and the priest interpreted, how one of them had heard in his mountain home that the American President who was at Paris had said that people should be free, should have a right to determine how and by whom they were to be governed. He wanted to be in Poland, not in Czechoslovakia, and so he had set out to walk to Paris to tell the President so.

On January 25, 1919, delegates from 27 countries filed into an imposing, ornately furnished chamber known as the Room of the Clock. They were there to discuss the League of Nations and to hear a speech by the American president. Wilson had insisted that the League be the first order of business, and Clemenceau and Lloyd George had consented. What else could they do? Wilson was still riding a crest of popularity and esteem.

From his place at the head table, the American president rose to speak. He began by impressing the delegates with the tragedy of war and set before them the possibility of an enduring peace. He said he knew the hearts of the common people, and they yearned for a League of Nations. "I have had the very delightful experience," Wilson said, "of visiting several nations since I came to this side of the water, and every time the voice of the body of the people reached me through any representative, at the front of its plea stood the hope for the League of Nations." He personally could never be party to a settlement that omitted a League, he said, because the American people demanded it and he was their servant. Further, he was under obligation to the American soldiers:

As I go about the streets here I see everywhere the American uniform. Those men came into the war after we had uttered our purposes. They came as crusaders, not merely to win a war, but to win a cause; and I am responsible for them, for it fell to me to formulate the purposes for which I asked them to fight, and I, like them, must be a crusader for these things, whatever it costs and whatever it may be necessary to do, in honor, to accomplish the object for which they fought.

When he was finished, the delegates all rose to applaud, and Colonel House scribbled a note, initialed it, and passed it along to the president's place. It read:

I believe that what you have said today will hearten the world as nothing you have said before. It was complete & satisfying—

EdwH

Wilson sent this message back:

We have got them all very solemnly and satisfactorily committed.

W.W.

And so they had. The League of Nations was all but adopted. After the president's speech, the conference appointed a special commission to draft a constitution for the League, a "covenant," as Wilson preferred to call it. But Wilson and House already had a satisfactory covenant in their pockets. The French members of the commission, under instructions from Clemenceau, could argue over its wording if they wished, but in all essentials it was to remain the president's kind of league, strong and just.

It was now February, and the Wilsons were preparing to leave for home. They would stay in Paris for the formal adoption of the League and then sail to America so that the president could attend the closing of Congress. But they would soon be back, because the world still needed Wilson to fight for the rest of his Fourteen Points.

True, there were some who were beginning to doubt the wisdom of the president's peace plan. In the cafes, they chuckled over a statement attributed to Clemenceau: "God Almighty gave to mankind the Ten Commandments—and we rejected them. Now comes Wilson with his Fourteen Points—we shall see!" But by most outward appearances, the president's prestige was as high as ever. Archie Taber, who saw Paris whenever he wasn't out testing airplanes, wrote home on February 7:

How simply amazing it is; the way all the civilized world looks at Wilson; the French look to him as they must have to Louis XIV or to Napoleon; I wonder if people in America appreciate the position he commands over here. To-day, walking down the Champs Elysees, I saw a long banner (at least fifty feet in length) inscribed thus:

HONNEUR A WILSON
le juste

I believe he will be known in history as "the Just," in the same way that we now speak of "Charles the Bold" or "John the Fearless."

The Paris peace conference of 27 nations met in the Room of the Clock on February 14 to vote on a League of

Nations. As usual, the session was closed to the public, but hidden away in a tiny alcove behind a heavy red curtain—a stowaway by special arrangement of Clemenceau himself—sat Mrs. Wilson. She peeked out through a crack in the curtains and heard her husband read off the 26 articles of the covenant and then explain to the delegates how the nations there assembled, by joining together in a league for peace and international cooperation, were doing something good and beautiful and epoch-making. From her seat behind the red curtain, Mrs. Wilson thought the speech "had made a great impression, and I longed to go to him and tell him all I felt." Finally, after the delegates had voted for the covenant and filed from the chamber, she rushed out into the street and found her husband waiting in the presidential car:

Oh, how glad I was to find him and tell him all the things that filled my heart!

He took off his high hat and leaned back in the car. "Are you so weary?" I asked. "Yes," he answered, "I suppose I am, but how little one man means when such vital things are at stake."

A row of soldiers saluted stiffly as the car started upon the first leg of the long journey home. Wilson smiled and said: "It will be sweet to go home, even for a few days, with the feeling that I have kept the faith with the people, particularly with these boys, God bless them."

13

THE PEACE THAT FAILED

"**R**ay, Ray, the Colonel is dead—Roosevelt!" shouted William Allen White, running up to a table in a Paris cafe, brandishing a newspaper and blinking back tears. Ray Stannard Baker stood and put his hand on White's shoulder. "Yes, Will, it's a great blow. We are all sorry." The two newspapermen sat down together and talked the rest of the morning about the loss of White's best friend, wondering what America would be like without him and agreeing that a good part of their world had died that day.

It was shocking; Roosevelt dead at 60 of a bad case of lumbago. You would have thought a man with Roosevelt's big muscular chest and whooping vitality might have fought off death as fiercely as he had once boxed, wrestled, hunted bears and campaigned for election. But odd as it seemed, Theodore Roosevelt had died in his sleep. There was no other news in America that day, only stories about the Colonel and famous old pictures of him riding a bulldozer in Panama, shaking his fist from a flag-draped speaker's platform, sitting on the carcass of an African buffalo he had shot and a close-up of him glowering at the camera, a determined patriotism bristling from every hair of his mustache. "America's best loved citizen gone!" mourned one newspaper editorial, and another echoed, "Farewell, O rare American." The date was January 7, 1919, only a week into the first year of what was supposed to be a splendid new era.

So the era had begun strangely and unhappily. Already events were taking a peculiar turn and the times seemed out of joint.

The biggest event of 1919 was supposed to be the return of the boys from "over there." Mothers and girlfriends dreamed of the juicy roasts and stews they would cook for the day of homecoming, and homesick soldiers dreamed of a hero's welcome. But somehow, few things worked out as expected. In early February, the Tabers of Princeton, New Jersey were telling neighbors how grateful they were that Archie had made it through the war. He loved flying, they said, and might even turn into a professional aviator upon his return home. He was expected home in March. But then one day a cable came from the government. It announced in stiff, official language that their son, Lieutenant Arthur Richmond Taber, had been killed while test-flying an army plane. The boy whom they had brought up to lead a manly life of adventure, self-sacrifice and humanitarian service was dead. He had been buried, said the army chaplain who had performed the ceremony, in a famous military cemetery across the Seine, under a simple wooden cross amidst the endless rows of war dead. Taps had sounded over his grave. A friend of Archie's wrote from France:

I cannot tell you how deeply I grieve with you about dear old Archie. I had been with him off and on since Ground-School at Princeton, and almost constantly for the past six months. He was my best friend over here . . . He was the finest boy I have ever known, and he had more respect, I think, of officers and men alike than any other officer on this post. He was so high-minded that at times he really made me ashamed of myself.

I was with him after lunch on the day of the accident . . . He was in such joyous spirits that day and just bubbling over with life.

I wish I could convey some idea of how wonderful I thought him—and everyone else did, too.

Devout Christians, the Tabers tried to accept Archie's death as the will of God; still, for them, the anticipated joys of 1919 had turned to sorrow and ashes.

Unlike the Tabers, most Americans had no tangible reason to feel bitter or unhappy with the postwar world. After all, 39 out of 40 of their sons in uniform had survived the Great War—a staggering percentage compared to the loss of one out of every five German soldiers and one out of every six Frenchmen.

True, it took a while for the wartime army to be demobilized. Half a year after the armistice, three-quarters of the boys were still in Europe waiting for ships to take them home. But by the time of the first frost in the fall of 1919, practically all of them had hung up their uniforms for good and returned to their hometown girls and their mothers' homecooked meals. Outwardly, then, 1919 was a good year. Still, one knew from the hollow feeling in the pit of the stomach that something was wrong.

It wasn't the cost of living, though the price of sugar was ridiculously high and going higher. It wasn't the labor unrest either, though working men were walking out of factories by the hundreds of thousands, striking for better pay. It was the boredom. Now that the war was over, there was nothing exciting left to do or think about. The Four-Minute Men in the local movie houses had no more rousing speeches to deliver. The Boy Scouts had no more pamphlets to distribute. And there were no more interesting battles and casualty lists to follow in the newspapers. The great letdown over the coming of peace had begun almost right away. Two days after the armistice, in fact, the *New York Tribunes*'s editorial read:

A stale, flat world we live in? No news worth reading, nothing worth doing except celebrating what is past and dead? Well, what else could anyone expect? We have been living on romance and adventure, the greatest adventure in the history of the world, for four years now. The morning's cup of coffee has been drunk to a daily accompaniment of colossal deeds that packed a newspaper's front page with headlines and crowded ordinary local doings off the stage altogether.

Such has been our scale of life and diet of excitement. Now, with a few strokes of a pen it is all withdrawn ...

It is a great slump we are going through, and we shall not gain anything by blinking our eyes to it . . . We find ourselves back in our old 1914 grooves—and we do not fit them—or if we do fit them they seem very shallow and straight and dull.

Many Americans discovered that one good way to get over being bored and disappointed with peace was to relive the war. They loved, for example, to hear Eddie Rickenbacker on his nationwide speaking tour tell stories about the 26 German planes he had shot down. Movie producers offered Eddie fabulous sums to re-enact his exploits on film, and vaudeville companies clamored for the chance to feature a genuine war hero on their summer tours. This is Rickenbacker's own description of the way the crowds greeted him in Los Angeles:

That Los Angeles celebration outdid them all. The official program had full-page advertisements from all the movie stars. The day began with a barbecue given by the Elks Lodge and attended by thousands. In the parade I rode in a mock-up of an airplane covered completely with flowers. It was stunningly beautiful, but I felt like an idiot riding in it for three hours.

From the ex-soldier's viewpoint, it was fun to be a war hero—for about a day. After that, it became a nuisance and a bore. The soldier, too, felt dissatisfied with postwar America. The daily habit of killing Germans or of lying in readiness thinking about killing them, had left an imprint on his mind. The experience had aged him. It was true what people said: He had left home a boy and returned a man. And the trouble was that he could never sit in the straw-backed rocker on the front porch of his parents' house with the same contentment as before. He felt restless with the quietness and dullness of home. An observer quoted in the *New York Times* remarked that he often overheard ex-soldiers talk fondly and longingly of war. In general, they felt:

"It wasn't so bad." They remember the comradeship of the life, the laughter they had even in Bad Places, the gay spirit

*of pals even in hours of imminent death. There were won-
derful "binges" out of the line in little French towns where
pretty girls were kind. It was a great adventure, where, if
a man was not afraid of death, he had lots of fun.*

*Peace looked enormously good when war was on, but now
it is rather drab, and something of the spice has gone out
of life.*

The white soldier had to adjust only to boredom; the black
soldier's adjustment was something far worse. Blacks came
home to an America that drew the color line as ruthlessly as
ever. There were the same lynchings and riots in 1919, only
more of them. The excuses, too, were familiar. In Washington, D.C. a white girl's report of having been assaulted by a
black man prompted white soldiers, sailors and marines to
roam the streets in search of black faces. The *New York
Times* reported on July 22, 1919:

*Late at night several negroes were attacked by soldiers
and marines at Fifteenth Street and New York Avenue . . .
within a stone's throw of the White House. Three negroes
beaten here were taken to the Third Precinct Police Station.*

*A band of soldiers and sailors dragged a young negro
from a street car on G Street, Northwest, between Ninth
and Tenth Streets. They beat him and chased him several
blocks. His head was cut . . .*

*A number of disturbances were caused by civilians who,
when a crowd of soldiers and sailors collected, pointed to
any negro who might be passing and yelled, "There he
goes!" Such outcries generally were followed by an attack
upon the negro by some of the soldiers and sailors.*

Washington's police force arrested ten men that night, two
whites and eight blacks.

Two weeks later, Chicago erupted. It was a stifling
summer afternoon, and the public beaches on Lake Mich-
igan were jammed. The black bathers sat on one side of
the beach and the white bathers on the other. In the water,
a black boy swam into what white boys considered their
territory. They started stoning the black boy. Blacks on
shore watched horrified as the boy sank and drowned.

Soon they leapt up and began hitting whites with fists and bottles. The race war spread inland until it engulfed all of Chicago. The war lasted a week, resulting in the deaths of 15 whites and 23 blacks. A month's peace, and then the races clashed again in Knoxville, Tennessee and again in Omaha, Nebraska and again in Elaine, Arkansas.

There were 75 lynchings in 1919, 10 more than in 1918. Many of the victims were ex-soldiers. Headlines like these were common in the black newspapers of 1919:

NEGRO KILLED IN HOSPITAL
Killed While Confined to Bed by Wounds

FORMER COLORED SOLDIER LYNCHED FOR HAVING WHITE SWEETHEART

FIFTH LYNCHING IN ARKANSAS
Sheriff Takes Man's Heart Home as a Souvenir
—Body Tied to an Automobile and Dragged
Through the Principal Streets

Black Americans had supported the war to the limit: 2,000,000 of their sons had gone into uniform, 10,000 had died in France; and this was their reward. They were bitter about it; they had a right to be bitter. Following the Washington riot, a large headline in the *Washington Bee* read:

THIS NATION'S GRATITUDE

THE COLORED AMERICANS' REWARD FOR FIGHTING FOR "WORLD DEMOCRACY"

INNOCENT COLORED CITIZENS ATTACKED —NO RESPECT FOR PERSONS OR PROPERTY—COLORED CITIZENS PULLED FROM STREET CARS AND ASSAULTED— POLICE DEPARTMENT APPEALED TO WITHOUT AVAIL

So the first year of peace was in no way a year of good will and brotherly love. To add to the tension of the racial crisis, other hostilities were beginning to flare across the nation. For long months, the American people had been taught to hate and fear a single enemy. Now that enemy had been defeated. But for many the anger and the hysteria did not stop with the end of the war. It was only redirected.

There were in the United States at the beginning of 1919 numbers of radicals who had openly sympathized with the revolution that had overthrown the czar in Russia. They looked upon communism as a hope for the world's future and were encouraged by its spread in Hungary, Germany and other parts of Europe. Thus, when Wilson sent American troops to Siberia in 1919 to reinforce Russian counter-revolutionaries in their bid to overthrow the new Bolshevik (Russian Communist) government, considerable radical protest ensued. This was in turn met with a strong reaction from conservative Americans, who developed a desperate fear of the possibility of a communist uprising in their country. The government responded by launching a series of investigations into the activities of aliens and citizens suspected of sympathies or connections with the communist cause. In the spate of violence that followed, several bombs wrapped in brown paper and made to look like parcels from Gimbels department store were sent to government officials and other prominent Americans. The bombs never reached their intended victims, but one of them blew off the hands of a servant and another killed a man. Given a new object for their fear and hatred, "patriotic" Americans reacted with a vengeance. When a radical in Indiana shouted, "To hell with the United States," a sailor pulled a gun and killed him. It took the jury two minutes to pronounce the sailor innocent of any crime. On May Day, as Socialists paraded in the streets of Cleveland, an army lieutenant stepped out of a group of soldiers, went up to one of the marchers and demanded that he throw away his red flag. The Socialist of course refused, and as the *New York Times* reported:

Immediately a free-for-all fight began, in which the soldiers were being badly handled, until the arrival of several policemen.

A hurry call for the reserves brought several mounted police, and they charged, driving their horses directly into the throng and swinging their clubs with good effect. A number of police horses were slashed with knives in the hands of the Socialists, while others pulled revolvers and fired at the police. The battle was so severe that fully twenty of the radicals were injured, some of them seriously . . .

The police had scarcely dispersed the throng in the square when another riot broke out two blocks away on Euclid Avenue, in the heart of the shopping district.

Women shoppers ran for shelter as the Socialists again fired, but the police, aided by soldiers, charged the throng. Windows in hotels, department stores and other buildings were crowded with spectators, who threw ink bottles, ink wells, sticks and other articles at the heads of the rioters in the streets below.

Socialist headquarters was totally wrecked when a throng of soldiers and civilians charged the place, driving the radicals out and completely demolishing the building. Typewriters and office furniture were thrown into the street.

This succession of clashes heightened the tension and ushered in one of the worst periods of suspicion and panic the country had ever seen. In a carryover from some of the repressive policies of wartime, the government struck blindly at aliens suspected of sympathies with the Bolsheviks. Thousands, including many American citizens and noncommunists, were arrested in the dead of night and herded into federal jails for trial and possible deportation. These unannounced roundups, known as the "Palmer raids" after the attorney general who planned them, ultimately resulted in the deportation of only 556 aliens, but they were one of the ugliest and most unfortunate legacies of the war.

And what of those who had been imprisoned for their opposition to the war? One year after the armistice, many socialists and Wobblies were still serving out long jail sentences for their antiwar positions. Liberal-minded men like Oswald Garrison Villard and the Reverend John Haynes Holmes tried to persuade President Wilson to declare a general amnesty for political prisoners. But the man who had spoken so passionately about democracy to European audiences refused.

Even before being shut away in the Atlanta Penitentiary, Eugene Debs had been in poor health. His body could not stand for long a prison diet of beans and dry bread. He was dying a slow death. But when somebody proposed that he could probably be pardoned if he took back his antiwar position, anger shot through his tall, bony frame. "Repent! Repent!" he exclaimed.

Repent for standing like a man! For having a conviction about a public question, and standing by it for a cause! Why, before I would don the sackcloth and get down into the ashes before the Attorney General or any other man on earth for having a principle I would gladly walk to the gallows or the stake.

Emma Goldman also remained defiant to the end. Her two-year jail sentence expired in the fall of 1919, just in time for her to be deported as a casualty of the Palmer raids. The federal dragnet swept up Emma Goldman and her friend Sasha almost as soon as they left their prison cells. Emma's quick tongue flailed the immigration officials in charge of her case, but, as in the past, the officials ruled against her. She reserved her bitterest words about the United States for the wintry day when she and Sasha and numerous other radicals were roused out of bed late at night and herded into a ship bound for Russia. As recorded in her autobiography:

The uniformed men stationed themselves along the walls, and then came the command: "Line up!" A sudden hush fell upon the room. "March!" It echoed through the corridor.

Deep snow lay on the ground; the air was cut by a biting wind. A row of armed civilians and soldiers stood along the road to the bank. Dimly the outlines of a barge were visible through the morning mist. One by one the deportees marched, flanked on each side by the uniformed men, curses and threats accompanying the thud of their feet on the frozen ground. When the last man had crossed the gangplank, the girls and I were ordered to follow, officers in front and in back of us.

We were led to a cabin. A large fire roared in the iron stove, filling the air with heat and fumes. We felt suffocated. There was no air nor water. Then came a violent lurch; we were on our way.

I looked at my watch. It was 4:20 A.M. on the day of our Lord, December 21, 1919. On the deck above us I could hear the men tramping up and down in the wintry blast. I felt dizzy, visioning a transport of politicals doomed to Siberia . . . Russia of the past rose before me and I saw the revolutionary martyrs being driven into exile. But no, it was New York, it was America, the land of liberty! Through the port-hole I could see the great city receding into the distance, its skyline of buildings traceable by their rearing heads. It was my beloved city, the metropolis of the New World. It was America indeed, America repeating the terrible scenes of tsarist Russia! I glanced up—the Statue of Liberty!

Seeing Gene Debs in jail and Emma Goldman deported for speaking their minds, Oswald Garrison Villard, John Haynes Holmes and other reflective Americans wondered what had become of the country they loved. Only five years before, Americans had spoken proudly of their tolerance and respect for a man's right to act according to his conscience. On armistice day, they had rejoiced about the dawning of a new golden age of man. Now, however, in this unusually colorless, rainy fall of 1919, it seemed that America's golden age lay not in the future but in the past. The ex-soldiers—toughened men whom people had once called "the boys"—knew this. The aggressive patriots, who had once found in Theodore Roosevelt the living proof of a vigorous and cocksure Americanism, knew it too. And black Americans knew it best of all.

Only Woodrow Wilson did not yet know. Wilson kept his faith in a beautiful new world after others all around him had either given it up an as illusion or lost interest.

First to weaken was his old friend Colonel House. Wilson had left House in charge of his Paris peace program for the month that he was away in America. The night he returned to Europe, he conferred eagerly with House. Mrs. Wilson remembered how he looked when he left that conference:

The change in his appearance shocked me. He seemed to have aged ten years, and his jaw was set in that way it had when he was making a superhuman effort to control himself. Silently he held out his hand, which I grasped, crying: "What is the matter? What has happened?"

He smiled bitterly. "House has given away everything I had won before we left Paris. He has compromised on every side, and so I have to start all over again . . . "

Grimly squaring his jaw, Wilson resolved to fight day and night until he retrieved the lost ground. But he never quite managed it. He worked as if driven by a demon, straining his health to the breaking point. He developed a nervous twitch; the muscles along one side of his face would contract in ugly spasms. Daily his condition grew worse.

Despite all Wilson's efforts, it proved impossible for a lone and ailing man to uphold his ideals against a clamoring host of selfish politicians. The treaty to which he at last consented looked more like a treaty of vengeance than a treaty of peace. It split off one section of Germany and gave it to Poland, severed another section and gave it to France. A third parcel of the old Germany went to Belgium and a fourth to Denmark. All told, the treaty shrank German territory by 25,000 square miles and her population by 9,000,000. With the land went more than half of Germany's iron supply and slightly under half of her coal. What coal remained could be demanded by the Allies as partial reparation for the $33 billion of war damages charged against Germany. The German army was to be reduced to 100,000 men, a force smaller than Switzerland's, and no German soldier could stand within 100 miles of the French border. Germany's most powerful ships of war would be transferred to the British navy, and she could not build replacements. She could have no air force whatsoever. On top of these crushing demands, there was a clause more hateful to the German people than any other suggesting that Germany alone was to blame for the world war.

Humiliated, bitter, resentful, Germany nonetheless signed the Treaty of Versailles because she had no choice. Wilson signed it, too. Unhappy though he was about its harshness, he was still proud of its first and most important part, the section creating a League of Nations. The League, he believed, would guarantee peace between nations. Germany's bitterness would fade with time, the scars of this war would heal, and there would never be another.

Wilson therefore held his head high when, on July 10, 1919, he presented the treaty to the Senate for its approval. In his speech he referred to the League of Nations as "the only hope for mankind," and suggested that America's acceptance of it was divinely foreordained:

The stage is set, the destiny disclosed. It has come about by no plan of our conceiving, but by the hand of God who led us into this way. We cannot turn back. We can only go forward, with lifted eyes and freshened spirit, to follow the vision. It was of this that we dreamed at our birth. America shall, in truth, show the way. The light streams upon the path ahead, and nowhere else.

Wilson was fully aware that the idealism of his speech soared over the heads of certain senators in his audience. He did not really like politicians, especially Republican politicians—and especially now that the Republicans were sniping at him unmercifully. They were calling him a dictator worse than the kaiser and saying that his League was an invitation to disaster. Some of the opposition was no more than the natural isolationism of men who had just seen their nation go to war and didn't wish her to be duty bound to go again. But there was also a measure of national self-interest in their disaffection with the League: As a signatory to such a peacekeeping organization, America would be restricted in her future foreign policy. This prospect was distasteful to many Republicans, particularly now that the United States was emerging from

World War I as a major economic and political power. Some senators threatened not to vote for the Treaty of Versailles unless Wilson watered down America's commitment to the League; others refused to accept even the weakest kind of commitment. In other words, the Republican senators meant either to cripple the League or to defeat it.

But Wilson refused to believe that this small group of politicians expressed the sentiments of the American people. Americans in the postwar world, he believed, were as high-minded as ever. In wartime he had called upon them to give money, energy and blood for democracy and mankind, and they had done it. Surely in peacetime, if he called upon them again to raise their voices for the same ideals, they would rally behind the League, and a stubborn Senate would be forced to accept it. So Wilson kept the faith.

On September 3, 1919, he boarded a train that was scheduled to take him almost 10,000 miles across the country and back, on the most ambitious and grueling speaking tour of his life. His doctor pleaded with him not to strain his health again, but Wilson insisted on going. "I do not want to do anything foolhardy," he said, "but the League of Nations is now in its crisis, and if it fails, I hate to think of what will happen to the world."

So the train bearing President and Mrs. Wilson pulled out of the Washington station, westward bound. The president spoke first at Columbus, Ohio and later the same day in Indianapolis, Indiana. Two days in Missouri, a day in Iowa, another in Minnesota, another in North Dakota— the train rattled on and on. Wilson's head throbbed the whole way, but he kept on speaking, twice a day. The League of Nations was America's supreme contribution to a better world, he said. It would pass the Senate because Americans believed in it. A day in Oregon, four in California. The train reversed direction, heading east. The speaking tour was more than half over. By now Wilson's head throbbed so badly he couldn't sleep. Mrs. Wilson begged him to rest for a few days. But Wilson said: "I have caught the imagination of the people. They are eager to hear what the League stands for. I should fail in my duty if I disappointed them." So it was on to Denver and then to Pueblo, Colorado. The Pueblo speech concluded:

I believe that men will see the truth, eye to eye and face to face. There is one thing that the American people always rise to and extend their hand to, and that is the truth of justice and of liberty and of peace. We have accepted that truth and we are going to be led by it, and it is going to lead us, and through us the world, out into pastures of quietness and peace such as the world never dreamed of before.

They were the last words Wilson would ever utter from a public platform. Early on the morning of September 26, 1919, as the train pulled into Wichita, Kansas for another speech, Mrs. Wilson found her husband in the sleeping car "piteously ill," the whole left side of his face a stiff and lifeless mass.

For a few days after returning to Washington, Wilson seemed to be recovering slowly, but then on the morning of October 2, his wife found him stretched out on the bathroom floor, unconscious. A blood clot had blocked off a portion of his heart and almost killed him. It might have been better if it had. Wilson awoke from days of unconsciousness to find one arm and one leg limp and unmoving, his whole left side paralyzed. A cripple and an old man at only 63, Wilson still devoted his thoughts and dreams to the League of Nations. But he was now powerless to do anything about it, except to whisper insistently to his wife and to Gilbert Hitchcock, the one Democratic senator who came to see him, that the Republicans must not be permitted to alter what had been done at Paris.

It was November 1919. The League was coming to a vote in the Senate. It was time that the American people rallied behind Wilson as they had rallied back in May 1915 after the *Lusitania* crisis, when the watchword everywhere was "Stand Behind the President," and again in February 1917 when Germany resumed submarine warfare, and again in April 1917 when the nation went to war, and yet again in June when young men registered for the draft. Now it was November 1919, and Wilson needed the people more than ever.

But 1919 was not 1915. These days, people had other things to do besides "standing behind the president" and raising their voices for a League of Nations. The price of sugar was outrageous; the boys had come back men; the steelworkers were out on strike; and people said the Communists were threatening to take over the country. Next to these things, a peacekeeping organization far away in Europe seemed remote and dull. Besides, there were many who, like the Republicans in Congress, were wondering whether America had any business in a League of Nations in the first place. Many Americans, therefore, felt neither shocked nor sorry when, on November 19, 1919, the League of Nations twice came to a vote in the Senate and twice was voted down. Not until 1921 did the United States sign its own separate peace with Germany as an independent belligerent, not as a member of the League.

The League was dead in America. Wilson, however, refused to recognize it. He looked forward to the next year's election, when the people would have the chance to turn the Republicans out of the Senate and endorse the Democratic presidential candidate, who, of course, would champion the League as he had. The Democrats did, in fact, pick a man who stood for Wilson's League, and the Republicans picked a man who stood for something called "normalcy." When a member of his cabinet predicted a Republican victory, Wilson responded, "Daniels, you haven't enough faith in the people!" But when the people went to the polls on November 2, 1920, they voted almost two to one for Warren G. Harding and "normalcy." After that, even Wilson knew that the League of Nations, the heart of his dream. for a peaceful world, was dead in America. And so a sick and broken man hobbled from the White House, forgotten.

Entering the 1920s, Americans became used to a world without Woodrow Wilson and Theodore Roosevelt and the hundred thousand boys like Archie Taber who never came back. They tried to forget about the past and especially about the war, and they stopped talking about the dawn of a new day when the whole world would know a democracy as good as America's. Instead of politics, they talked now about a glittering array of new amusements and fads—new dance steps like the Black Bottom and the Charleston, new automobiles, new ways to make gin in your bathtub, a new record for flagpole sitting and—the greatest rage of all—a new invention called the radio.

Occasionally, reminders of the past intruded. Every November 11, for example, there were Armistice Day parades. And one February morning in 1924, Americans read in the newspapers that Woodrow Wilson had died. At moments like this, they remembered a time when people talked seriously of a world without war and when the whole world seemed to look to America to show the way to a just and lasting peace. But that time was past. Old dreams were dead. Americans had seen peace fail in 1914, and they fully expected to see it fail again. So they returned to their jobs, found new amusements, listened to jazz on the radio and tried to forget about the America they had lost.

EPILOGUE
Past Choices . . .
Current Choices

The 1914–1919 struggle was known by various names. In 1914 it was called the European War or the Great War. Soon it became the World War and "the war to end all wars." Since 1939–1945, when the struggle was repeated on the same vast scale, it has been known as World War I, thus fixing its place in history as simply the first of two great 20th-century struggles.

World War I marked the end of many things and the beginning of many others. It dissolved the Austro-Hungarian empire and created Czechslovakia and Yugoslavia as new states. It stripped Germany of territory on its eastern and western borders. It established a free Poland. It brought about the fall of the kaiser in Germany and the tsar in Russia. It resulted in the founding of the League of Nations. It brought continued suffering to uncounted millions. For good or ill these were the major immediate consequences of World War I.

To understand the meaning of the war we need to try to see it through the eyes of those who lived through it or were engulfed by it—Americans who woke up to the news of the *Lusitania* sinking, housewives who baked Liberty Bread, men who bought Liberty Bonds, soldiers who fought at Belleau Woods, blacks who were massacred at East St. Louis, Socialists who were jailed under the Espionage Act. For some it was America's finest hour; for others it was her darkest.

After peace returned some continued to believe that America's participation in the war was a moment unsurpassed in its history. America had a higher reason for war (these people believed) than simply upholding national "honor" against German insults. Germany had shown itself as an enemy of mankind by violating Belgian neutrality, shooting Belgian woman and children, and burning whole villages to the ground. This and unrestricted submarine warfare was not the "decent" warfare of soldier against soldier, but wanton butchery. America entered the war to put an end to such outrages. In declaring war Wilson had truly believed that he was placing before Americans the chance to make the world safe for democracy. The response of the American people supported this claim. Americans achieved in 18 months what the European powers had been unable to do in four years—they put an end to the war. For one brief moment from April 1917 to November 1918 there was no prouder thing on earth than to be able to call oneself an American.

To others the struggle remained a dirty, tragic affair. It began only because Europe's bankers and manufacturers maneuvered their respective governments and peoples into armed conflict with their enemies and rivals. Wilson himself maneuvered a naive and patriotic people into a war not for national honor or neutral rights or a democratic world, but for the protection of the selfish interests of American manufacturers, bankers and wartime profiteers. Wilson did nothing to improve the lot of black Americans; he rode roughshod over human liberties with a Selective Service Act that deprived everybody of freedom of body and of mind and an Espionage Act that deprived everybody of freedom of speech.

People carried over into peacetime the ruthless intolerance that the war had taught them to practice so well. In 1918 they mobbed and jailed Wobblies and Socialists whose criticism of the government was labeled treason. In 1919 they clamored to have these same radicals driven out of the country. In 1916 Reverend John Haynes Holmes had warned that once we went to war "our mission as a nation is at an end." Only a year after the armistice he watched his prophesy come true as the American people stood passively by while the League of Nations, the one thing that many believed would redeem the bloodshed and horror of the war, went down in defeat in the Senate. Evidently it was far easier for Americans to commit themselves to war than to a struggle for an enduring peace. The tragedy was all the greater in the light of what might have been. If the United States had stayed out of the war it would have strengthened its claim as a champion of world peace. The quality of American life and leadership might have continued to progress.

Was America's experience in World War I the tragedy that Ernest Meyer and others said it was? Or was it, as Theodore Roosevelt believed, a triumph of American idealism? The question has a continuing importance not only for Americans but for many others. World War I did more than usher in the 20th century; the study of this conflict is one of the keys to the history of the century itself.

BIBLIOGRAPHY

ORIGINS OF THE WAR IN EUROPE

A clear, concise account of the events and circumstances leading to war is Joachim Remak's *The Origins of World War I, 1871–1914*, New York, Holt, Rinehart & Winston, 1967. Other historians, while treating diverse causes, single out one as the most decisive. In *The Long Fuse: An Interpretation of the Origins of World War I*, New York, Lippincott, 1971, Laurence Lafore argues brilliantly that the only insoluble problem in Europe was the restless nationalism of the Serbs, Croats and others within the Austro-Hungarian empire. A German historian places the blame for war on the military and political leaders of his own country; see Fritz Fischer, *Germany's Aims in the First World War*, New York, Norton, 1961.

Building upon the insights of Lafore and Fischer is a scholarly analysis by James Joll in *The Origins of the First World War*, New York, Longman, 1984.

BIOGRAPHIES, LETTERS AND PERSONAL NARRATIVES

In any history of the American experience in World War I, Woodrow Wilson is a central figure. The passionate side of his complex personality is amply revealed in the letters collected in Woodrow Wilson, *A President in Love, The Courtship Letters of Woodrow Wilson and Edith Bolling Galt*, Boston, Houghton Mifflin, 1981. The tragedy of a crippled and defeated president after his stroke in 1919 is magnificently told in Gene Smith's When the Cheering Stopped: The Last Years of Woodrow Wilson, New York, Morrow, 1964. A short, readable biography of Wilson, which fairly treats his life and leadership, is Kendrick A. Clements' *Woodrow Wilson: World Statesman*, Boston, Twayne Publishers, 1987. For a more detailed treatment of Wilson's politics, see two fine biographies by Arthur S. Link: *Wilson: The Struggle for Neutrality, 1914–1915*, Princeton, Princeton University Press, 1960, and Wilson: *Campaigns for Progressivism and Peace, 1916–1917*, same publisher, 1965.

For the full story behind the jailing of Eugene Debs for his antiwar protests, read the concluding chapters of Nick Salvatore's *Eugene V. Debs: Citizen and Socialist*, Urbana, University of Illinois Press, 1982. The first chapter of Martha Solomon's *Emma Goldman*, Boston Twayne Publishers, 1987 describes the defiant spirit and titanic energies of one of history's most remarkable dissenters.

Thousands of those who fought on the Western Front published their war diaries, journals and letters home. Archie Taber's letters, for example, were privately printed by his family. More accessible to the general reader are the daily jottings of a young officer who barely survived a mad dash across no man's land: Edwin Campion Vaughan, *Some Desperate Glory: The World War I Diary of a British Officer, 1917*, New York, Henry Holt, 1981. Another first-person account is the entertaining autobiography by Edward V. Rickenbacker, *Rickenbacker*, Englewood Cliffs, N.J., Prentice-Hall, 1967.

THE WAR IN LITERATURE

For many young men in the trenches, the emotional experience of seeing death firsthand could only be expressed through poetry. The best of the British soldiers' poems have been collected in Dominic Hibberd and John Onions' *Poetry of the Great War: an Anthology*, New York, St. Martin's Press, 1986.

Among the hundreds of novels to emerge from the war, three have endured as classics: John Dos Passos, *Three Soldiers*, New York, George H. Doran Co., 1921; Ernest

Hemingway, *A Farewell to Arms*, New York, Scribner, 1929; and Erich Maria Remarque, *All Quiet on the Western Front*, Boston: Little, Brown, 1929. Though Remarque fought as a German and Dos Passos as an American, the stories they tell of the brutal, spirit-crushing effects of war are strikingly similar.

U.S. FOREIGN POLICY, 1914–1917

If President Wilson was committed to peace and neutrality, as he claimed, how was he finally persuaded to lead the United States to war? A deft analysis of Wilson's thinking is the brief diplomatic history by Arthur S. Link, *Wilson the Diplomatist*, Baltimore, The Johns Hopkins Press, 1957. A longer, more detailed history by Patrick Devlin—*Too Proud to Fight: Woodrow Wilson's Neutrality*, New York, Oxford University Press, 1975—argues that Wilson's personality strongly influenced his policies. See also the middle chapters of Page Smith, *America Enters the World: A People's History of the Progressive Era and World War I*, New York, McGraw-Hill, 1985, for a lucid narrative.

Focusing on a single episode, a splendid little book by Barbara Tuchman—*The Zimmermann Telegram*, New York, Macmillan, 1966—tells the suspenseful story of the decoding of German diplomatic messages by the British and its impact on American foreign policy.

FIGHTING THE WAR: MILITARY CAMPAIGNS

The calculations and miscalculations of the war's generals and admirals are thoroughly revealed in a vast number of military histories. For vivid illustrations (maps, posters, paintings, photographs) as well as a strong narrative, see Barnett Correlli's *The Great War*, New York, Putnam, 1980. Much briefer but unillustrated is James L. Stokesbury, *A Short History of World War I*, New York, Morrow, 1981. Submarine attacks and naval battles, including the decisive British victory at Jutland, are well described in Richard Hough, *The Great War at Sea 1914–1918*, New York, Oxford University Press, 1983. For a single-volume account of American troops "over there," nothing has surpassed the work of World War I veteran Laurence Stallings in *The Doughboys, the Story of the AEF, 1917–1918*, New York, Harper & Row, 1963.

Barbara Tuchman makes a compelling drama of the war's first month in her brilliant history *The Guns of August*, New York, Macmillan, 1962. The war's last year is also admirably described in John Toland, *No Man's Land: 1918, the Last Year of the Great War*, New York, Doubleday, 1980.

IMPACT OF THE WAR ON U.S. POLICY

This book focused more on the civilian's experience at home than the soldier's experience in the trenches. A readable and comprehensive account of the home front is Allen Churchill's *Over Here*, New York, Dodd, Mead, 1968. More challenging—but also rewarding—are the six essays on wartime society in David M. Kennedy's *Over Here: The First World War and American Society*, New York, Oxford University Press, 1980. Kennedy's first essay, "The War for the American Mind," exposes the negative impact of war on civil liberties and progressive politics. How wartime agencies such as the Food Administration regulated American society as never before is fully described in Robert H. Ferrell, *Woodrow Wilson and World War I*, New York, Harper & Row, 1985.

For a detailed account of the Socialists and conscientious objectors who were jailed for their antiwar acts, see Horace Peterson and Gilbert Fite, *Opponents of War, 1917–1918*, Seattle University of Washington Press, 1968. The racism and segregation policies of the U.S. Army and the Wilson administration are well documented in an excellent history of the black experience during the war: Arthur E. Barbeau and Florette Henri, *The Unknown Soldiers: Black American Troops in World War I*, Philadelphia, Temple University Press, 1974.

THE PARIS PEACE CONFERENCE

In *The End of Order: Versailles, 1919*, New York, Dutton, 180, Charles L. Mee Jr. uses war's devastation as the unforgettable and unforgivable backdrop to peace talks and explains in vivid prose why the diplomats at Paris created a treaty that was more vengeful than wise.

Also descriptive and illuminating is a shorter work by George Goldberg, *The Paris Peace Conference of 1919*, New York, Harcourt, Brace & World, 1969. For a detailed study of Wilson's leadership at Versailles, see Arthur Walworth, *Wilson and His Peacemakers: American Diplomacy at the Paris Peace Conference*, New York, Morton, 1984.

INDEX

STEVEN JANTZEN has earned degrees in American history and education from Dartmouth College, Harvard University and Princeton University. He wrote the original edition of his first book, *Hooray for Peace, Hurrah for War*, while studying for an advanced degree at Princeton. His career since then has focused on writing and editing textbooks for high school students. He has written and published numerous texts in history and government, including *American Adventures, World History: Perspectives on the Past* and *Government for Everybody*. He lives in New Jersey.

Jantzen, Steven

Hooray for peace, hurrah
for war: the United States
during World War I.